HOW TO SURVIVE IN
STAFFORDSHIRE

CHARLES WOOD

HALSGROVE

For Alina and my children with love

Other books by the author:

How To Survive In Somerset
Surviving Another Somerset Year
Exmoor Amour
Bats, Pads and Cider
Bats, Pads and Gladiators
Another Somerset Century
Bats and Belters – a novel

First published in Great Britain in 2016

Copyright © Charles Wood 2016
Illustrated by the Author

Publisher's Disclaimer
As is well known, Halsgrove have disowned Mr Wood on many occasions in the past and this particular volume is no exception. The views expressed herein arise entirely from the fevered brain of Mr Wood who remains entirely responsible for them, the Publisher is pleased to say.

British Library Cataloguing-in-Publication Data
A CIP record for this title is available from the British Library

ISBN 978 0 85704 300 9

HALSGROVE
Halsgrove House,
Ryelands Business Park,
Bagley Road, Wellington, Somerset TA21 9PZ
Tel: 01823 653777   Fax: 01823 216796
email: sales@halsgrove.com

Part of the Halsgrove group of companies
Information on all Halsgrove titles is available at: www.halsgrove.com

Printed and bound in China by Everbest Printing Investment Ltd

Naming of Parts

	Acknowledgements	4
LESSON ONE	Distant Beginning	5
LESSON TWO	Landlocked and Confusing	11
LESSON THREE	Learning Prudence	17
LESSON FOUR	Rhino, Peel and Chips	27
LESSON FIVE	Bull and Native Words	36
LESSON SIX	Bobble Hat and Strumpet	51
LESSON SEVEN	Oatcake, Hoof and Cut	63
LESSON EIGHT	Horn and Bladder	72
LESSON NINE	Flat Cap and Needle	77
LESSON TEN	Heroes and Arrows	88
LESSON ELEVEN	Bus and Armadillo	94
LESSON TWELVE	Shocks and Paint Pot	105
LESSON THIRTEEN	Parrot and Void	111
LESSON FOURTEEN	Paws and Pigman	117
LESSON FIFTEEN	Cheese and Chariot	126
LESSON SIXTEEN	Teapot and Radish	134
	Postscript	145
	Appendix One	147
	Appendix Two	149
	Appendix Three	152

Acknowledgements

My grateful thanks to Steven Pugsley and Julian Davidson at that edifice of publishing to let me just get on with it, safe in the knowledge that I've been 'surviving' for years. Sometimes personal experience can have positive effects even when occasionally it cuts a little near the bone.

With nothing being possible without the help of friends I am especially grateful to Romi, Monica, Mark, Anita, and Wild John, and to the others who might modestly introduce themselves in places herein. A bundle of thanks also to Lee Brown and I'm Too Old For This Malarky Part One and Part Deux.

Closer to home, I have to thank my lovely Alina for translating my English into English, and making my survival a joy. For my children Lawrence, Maddy, Ez and Felix who have had tough times, and whose support over the years has been an inspiration, I can only extend wonder, heartfelt love and gratitude.

Distant Beginning

"Prolonged endurance tames the bold."
Lord Byron, poet.

Melbourne sat behind me further than any potter could throw a mug. And there was risk of a Staffie tripping over a badger.

Countless stars shone the right way up above an expanse of wild considerably vaster than Cannock Chase. Yet the dark-skied West Country was suffering its annual moments of light pollution. A moth, hairy as a Bagot goat, bopped powdered wings into brightness. High in the village hall's apex ceiling florescent tubes harshly blazed on the sleep-fuggled senses. By my reckoning, it was a little after stupid o'clock. 3:15 according to my mobile. An hour fit only for creatures of talon and paw.

A table heaved with state-of-the-art GPS technology. A computer screen glared.

On a sturdier table: the trophy – a gurt lump of oak, carved into beseeching hands holding a compass to the sky.

Beneath a mounted and dusty, glazed-eyed, red deer stag's head, double doors were open to the mid-October night. Beyond, one of the toughest annual endurance events in the UK – the 'Exmoor 30:30'. Thirty pounds of weight per person is carried over 30 miles in a 'fast walk' paratroopers' call a 'tab' and marines, a 'yomp'.

Eleven teams were up for it in 2015. All were raising money for the Royal British Legion to help provide welfare for the serving and ex-service community and their families. Here were former military and insane civilians, guys and gals, some over fifties and, remarkably, three teams of sprogs from Uttox-eter's Denstone College.

Past winners of the event, the college was again among the favourites. Put it down to adventurous spirit. Gorblimey, for the school to produce a team of sixteen teachers and students that ringed three thousand birds on Inaccessible Island, a five and a bit square mile extinct volcano in the South Atlantic, there had to be a certain pedigree. Imagine trotting after the Inaccessible rail – Atlantisia rogersi – the world's smallest living flightless bundle of feathers, its legs adapted for pegging it.

Heads warmed by cosy beanies or Himalayan wool hats, competitors mingled with local insomniacs and jetlagged me. Yearning coffee I spared a thought for the inevitable blistered feet, tortured muscles, and laboured breath of others.

Amid a quiet hubbub of preparation yawned nine of Burntwood's finest. Which, to give a sense of location, is where a harvest of Anglo-Saxon gold and silver, so beautiful it bought tears to the eyes of one expert, poured out of a farmer's potato field – the largest hoard of period gold ever found. Yes, bigger than Suffolk's Sutton Hoo. Nothing feminine, mind. Everything was war gear: a gold hilt fitting with inlaid garnets, a gold animal figure helmet crest, gold scabbard strips with biblical inscriptions, gold helmet cheek pieces – the sort of stuff to cause a run on sales of metal detectors.

Or, to put Burntwood's location alternatively, it's Lichfield way.

Let me elaborate. Staffs currently resembles a pigeon-pecked wilted lettuce whose head's capped by Cheshire and Derbyshire, given an easterly kiss by Leicestershire, and whose stalk is rooted in Shropshire, Worcestershire ... and somewhere new-fangled.

Inside its county boundary Staffs boasts nine districts. East to west, the upper three are the rugged Staffordshire Moorlands, the urban sprawling City of Stoke-on-Trent, and Newcastle-under-Lyme. East Staffordshire and Stafford lie low and make up the middle. And of the bottom four, titchy Tamworth is clamped like a ball in a dog's maw by Lichfield, which in turn squeezes lovely Cannock Chase against South Staffordshire, the aforesaid lettuce stalk. Clear as crystal?

The Malarkeys, presenting as a pair of teams a hundred and eighty miles from home, vied for twelve-month bragging rights. A Royal Navy versus Army kind of affair. Paul, Steve, and Francois, matelot charmed, bribed by plentiful pints, sucked-in Pedigree tums. Chirpy team leader Lee Brown drew in his little Guinness gut. And soppy grins were held for the nanosecond of camera flash.

Next to pose, the opposition. Bald as a Chasewater coot, their team leader, Dick Whittington, had copied Lee's recruiting tactics for the good of the 'Army'. Oh dear, Lee and Dick. Familiar faces from previous years the two mates rivalry is nothing short of epic and both have a slightly skewed way of seeing the world.

Understandable, really.

Why? Look no further than the bushy-tailed squaddies, my son included, 'passing out' from basic training at Lichfield barracks. Daily ordered from the warm comfort and safety of their 'gonk-bags' they have choked, cried, vomited, collapsed, or peed themselves; run oodles carrying more kit than is entirely necessary; and been verbally abused by their corporals. None will ever forget to change their socks, shave their face, or clean their weapon. Some will make the ultimate sacrifice.

Rather than pull strings in life, Lee sawed them with a strung horsehair bow. Not the Robin Hood sort. Lee's double bass miaowed deeply at concert-goers both sides of the 'Pond', be they in a pew-filled Lichfield Cathedral or in a throng of New Yorkers at the foot of the World Trade Center.

At heart, though, Lee's a sailor. Crotchets and quavers left in his wake, he cut waters more hazardous than Chasewater's ripples and faced dangers greater than tufted ducks and carnivorous broad-leafed sundew. Hazards not quite as big, mind you, as the iceberg faced by Staffordshire's most famous sea dog, Edward Smith. From Hanley, he was skipper of the *Titanic*, and about whom on 26 April 1912 the *Lichfield Mercury* reported: "the words of the captain, 'Be British', showed how bravely a man could die".

Dick, on the other hand, did is best to keep clear of being in deep water and oddly sought to protect sods and sands lacking coal and useless for pots. His and Lee's banter never lets up. Indeed, Dick's folklore namesake gave Lee fodder to josh: "if you're missing a pussy-cat, Dick, cuddle the Exmoor Beast."

The riposte was quick as broadband. "Seen the Stoke City mascot, the fat hippo Pottermus? Reckon it's your role model." Sniggers from Dick's loyal bunch: Neil, Richard, Spence and Craig. The latter, soft-whiskered and wearing a generous white tee-shirt, which bore the message 'Live On' and printed with a red remembrance poppy, gave his fag packet a reassuring pat. A pair of walking poles clattered. "Christsakes Spence, you'll wake the pheasant millions," muttered Craig, out the corner of his mouth.

Absolutely, I thought. Dangerous birds fezzies, if startled. They tend to zoom directionless. Staffordshire had proof attesting to it. Although, best I kept shtum about that scary nugget until it was more appropriate. I did, however, sidle up and mention George, a territorial bird so aggressive that the Wootton postman armed himself with a stick on his rounds. A helpful local had suggested opening an umbrella in the fezzie's face to "scare the bejeezus out of him". Through trial and error, raisins soaked in rum did the pacifying job.

Craig snapped himself a square of mint cake and turned to look Spence in the eye. "Got any raisins in yer hip flask? And gotta say it, in them three-quarter lengths you risk Lyme disease. Suss, Spence? Deer ticks? They have 'em here too, yer know. Lots of 'em. Haven't yer learnt that yet?" True enough. The opportunist mini body burrowers would likely be leaping hoop-la from bracken fern at Spence's bared calves.

"A cotton reel's what's needed," I chirped. "Rip off a length of thread, lasso it around the little bugger's body, tighten, then pull slowly. It'll come out body, legs, and all. Easy-peasy."

"Phrrrr. I'll remember for next year," Spence mumbled. Good he tweaked his ear stud for luck.

The camera flashed again. The team photos done for the record, a tall and lean flat-cap with SAS credentials hollered. "Thirty seconds, 'I'm Too Old For This Malarkey'! Two minutes 'I'm Too Old For This Malarkey … Part Deux'!"

"Chests out, you swobsy lot! You're from the creative county!" ejaculated Dick.

"Blessed are the short-winded, for they shall be invited back!" Lee heckled. Collective laughter.

Backpacks, each with a tracking device shoved inside, had final strap adjustments until degrees of individual comfort were discovered. Knees bowed. Glow sticks dangled. Head-torches got flicked on apart from one or two tinkered with. Maps received last squints. Sotto voce and happy as a porker in poo Paul continued Dutch Francois' education of 'Ar ter toke crate'.

Finally, to volleys of rallying applause and all foreheads beaming the two sets of Malarkeys, minimally apart, were loose. The initial 2-mile steep hill climb from village to ancient burial mound on the high moor was knacker-ing. The race's flat-capped organiser-in-chief couldn't restrain a chuckle at distant expletives. What a hill it was to cause such freedom of expression.

An owl made a low query. "Knotters, that's who. Fab, innit?" I answered. Ah, the wondrous Stafford knot. The distinctive three-looper. Staffordshire's traditional symbol appears everywhere in the creative county. From road signs and milk cartons to university and county cricket club crests. And this was because a cost conscience hangman once came up with a way to dispatch three unsavoury souls with a single length of rope. Unedifying.

"What is it with you and Staffs? Former life as a saggar maker's bottom knocker?"

The accent over my shoulder was familiar.

"Could well have had." I hoped to sound enigmatic. Bashing out lumps of coarse local clay inside an iron hoop gave a nipper his job title. He made the base of the saggar – the large clay vessel used to contain the pottery ware for firing.

The accent belonged to Hednesford-born paramedic Gary. Wales had lately adopted him. Little different to Staffs embracing Shropshire's Charles Darwin, I suppose. "Crazy thing," said Gary, "some in those two Malarkey crews might even have gone to the same school as me. Funny as hell, think-ing that. Have any of 'em matched your love of Stoke City?"

"Whoa. Don't label me. Evenings at altitude have been spent hyperther-mic in Burslem rattling a rattle for Port Vale."

Gary tugged his spectacles to the end of his nose and over them gave me a look of pity. "Know what mate? With you being such a bloody Staffs romantic you should write a survival guide. You can include that story of the haunted radish you bang on about. And you can confess to the world your old university mascot's a boot-scraper."

"Oi, don't malign Herbert." Hell's teeth. Agreed Herbert the Dragon had been a boot-scraper, a big one, and was totted from a rubbish tip. But at his best Herbert had scraped the mucky soles of blue bloods. And when his bronze body was polished he looked as lovely and fantastical as Copenhagen's 'Little Mermaid', or Black Mere's for that matter. "Herbert's legendary," I said.

"Maybe to a lesser extent than the Rudyard Lake lioness up on YouTube. With lots of lovely woodland to pather in she's likely got big pussy cat friends..." Gary tailed off, probably aware of my faraway look. "Hmm. I'll leave you to your thoughts. Word of warning, don't forget Burton Albion."

"Potters, Valiants, and Brewers. Noted," I said, adding, "Just think, had that lioness been around in the 1860s she would have put-off thousands of day-trippers. John Kipling and Alice Macdonald might never have seen their love blossom. No son called Rudyard. And life without *The Jungle Book*. Golly."

"Ha-bloody-ha. Lacking an airport, for a Staffie to go anywhere exotic is a bugbear. I say it as it is: the county's barren in the north, good only for spuds and cows in the middle, and too near Brum in the south. Gotta go. Duty calls."

And perhaps for a time 'duty' did. Come daybreak, however, race paparazzi snapped the 'Welshman' mouth agape and drooling, asleep in the front seat of the race ambulance thronged by tangle-fleeced sheep.

But, fair to say, Gary's seed germinated over a breakfast fry-up. The idea had pith. Jaunts around the county stirred creativity. Secrets got discovered. The Malarkeys were but the value added.

Their Chasewater link for instance jogged my memory to when I randomly followed an overgrown stony track bed. The remnants of the lake's rail connection that fell victim to the 1965 Beeching Axe, it led me to a high metal footbridge joining the ghost platforms of Hammerwich station. The lonely vision in rural nowhere offered little more than heady sparrow-eye views for clambering rabbits. And just for them, I found out, it's kept in safe nick by network rail. Spurred on, I impulsively tracked a fruitful branch of my family tree to a slot machine museum.

Then there were friends, the rooted characters. Those like Stewy the Bog Snorkler and Teapot Liz. Happily winkled out in Staffordshire towns, they and their ilk were rare as rocking horse shit on new-fangled Facebook.

Undoubtedly there are sounder reasons to write. Thinking big might inspire whacking up a Brasilia of the Potteries. Marvellous things are achieved against the odds. Never lose sight of the DNA double helix, penicillin, and the Internet being hit on by bods having a laugh.

But actually, perhaps being quietly informative would suffice. Like drawing attention to Lichfield's city drunk Sarah Thacker who in 1886 was given fourteen days' in gaol with hard labour, her thirtieth such conviction; or to the city in 1938 having "the eyes of Europe" on it when testing the "most effective street-lighting and air-raid control system known to modern science"; or, indeed, to the city's crumbling clock tower ravaged by death-watch beetles in recent years suffering clock dial attacks from airguns.

Calculating a probable nine hours until the first Malarkey flopped across the finish line probably well behind any Denstone intrepid, I had oodles of time to check even my pheasant facts and start finger tapping.

Where to begin?

Comparisons maybe. I had one for starters. Whereas the London Shard at well over a thousand feet high has a tremendous modish footprint amongst extremely valuable real estate, the Tunstall Shard at thirty-five feet has a monstrous 'Roman' fingerprint set amongst the much lesser dear. Hmm. A three hundred times enlargement of a piece of old pottery doesn't really grab the attention.

I decided on gauging character. Best be pragmatic. I plumped for something in Rugeley as illustrative.

Over a grave inside the cemetery's weathered brick perimeter wall, close to a couple of yew trees, one sizably older than the other, stands a tall, bare-foot gothic curiosity from 1944. Divertingly curvaceous, it's an melancholy angel. Wings folded, a revealing shift hugs her thighs and a hand loosely holds a floral spray. Below sumptuous curls her eyes are lowered to the inscription: 'Deadman'. There you have it. Over embellished maybe, but being matter-of-fact is a habit. Staffordshire folk, Gary included, just can't help themselves...

Landlocked and Confusing

"Change brings opportunities.
On the other hand, change can be confusing."

Michael Porter, economist.

1979

Really, had I a double infusion of quality Staffordshire blood? It was a knotty question borne out of idle teenage rumination.

Squidged on the damp sitting room bookshelf was a handed down off-putting mildewed hardback. Published in 1912, its author was Frank Falkner; it's full title: *The Wood Family of Burslem – A brief biography of those of its members who were sculptors modellers and potters.*

"Brim full of our lots peasant pottery and figurines" was how my dad, Maurice, described the tome. 'Our lots'? It was a tantalising titbit. And there were others.

"Past Woods liked playing with clay," Dad said, when at the age of six I produced a crude Plasticine dog.

Caught cleaning out the goldfish with something I shouldn't he offered: "Ralph Wood junior introduced the Toby jug." The beer mug, in the shape of a stout old man wearing a tricorn hat, had its origins in an eighteenth-century poem about a drink-loving soldier called Toby Philpot. The pun was obvious.

When ambling passed a Methodist chapel Dad imparted further wisdom. "Enoch Wood made the definitive bust of Thomas Wesley."

And around my twelfth birthday, hoping he hadn't "put two and two together and made seven", Dad produced a sheet of A4. On it a family tree in careful pencil. I saw Enoch's name. Dad had labelled him 'Father of the Potteries' and suggested that I could "humbly admit with greater chance than Staffordshire being elevated to a first class cricket county" to belonging to the man's line. I recall the nugget went in one ear and out the other. He also mentioned, I'm pretty sure, that the Toby jug Wood's ma went for a potter. I took it she wed a Wedgwood rather than let Mow Cop stretch her legs.

It was only in the autumn days before going up to university when our damp West Country house proved attractive to the small and industrious that I discovered that mum, who's maiden name was Peel, had curiously relevant Staffs ties too.

Slugs having set an invasive precedent, country mice began manufacturing a portal into the kitchen. Their groundwork audible in the most awkward of places Dad quit riffling through fusty, dog-eared documents and emerged from out from his pipe-smoke miasma to issue orders.

The Queen Anne vintage sideboard, an unnecessarily heavy lump of dark oak, had to be shifted. Before doing so, the Wedgwood willow pattern dinner service on display needed making safe. Each piece bearing the potter's mark had to be individually wrapped. Sheets of month old *Daily Telegraphs* sufficed for the job. 'Somalia Adopts Constitution' was perfect news for a dinner plate. 'The Ford Cortina, Britain's best-selling car, receives a major facelift', was ample for a porridge bowl. While 'Letters to the Editor: Brighton's nudist beach' was worthy of the gravy boat. Its bottom bore the word 'WEDGE-WOOD'. The middle 'E' was especially naughty. Manufactured by rascals William Smith & Co., they were Yorkshire tykes trying to pass their stuff off as being proper. Gran had fallen for it. But this wasn't something mentioned when we had guests.

'Stoke City 3 Tottenham Hotspur 1.' A sports page caused me to pause in bundling up the authentic china meat platter. A brace from 'cocky' son of Bucknall, Garth Crooks, and a Brendan O'Callaghan thump 'lifts the Victoria Ground roof'. Cor, and I would be soon be in those stands myself. The very idea gave me the tingles.

On the opposite page it was still cricket season. 'At a soggy Sandwell Park, West Bromwich, after following-on, Staffordshire get away with a draw against Durham in Minor Counties Championship.' This prompted a question. And an England without Wikipedia meant relying on the available fount of knowledge.

"Dad, is West Bromwich in Staffordshire?"

Pregnant pause. "Don't ask stupid questions, boy." A standard response when he hadn't the foggiest.

"Well, what about 'Wulfrunians'?" Ooh, the word could be phruffed and puffed over and over as private entertainment. 'Wull-fff-run-nians'. "Geography-wise Wolverhampton's higher than West Brom. Are Wulfrunians Staffies?"

A heavy paternal sigh and reddening ears meant Dad really hadn't a clue. "They *might* be *historically*," he stabbed in the dark. Pretty damned accurately, to be fair.

To coin Wolverhampton's motto: 'out of darkness cometh light'. Indeed, indeed. During his journey on HMS *Beagle* Charles Darwin, casting around for analogy, compared South America's volcanic chimneys spouting steam and smoke to "Wolverhampton's furnaces". At that moment those furnaces definitely were Staffordshire's.

Now the truth is out. Staffs is landlocked and prone to shrinkage. Natives' joke that, further political tinkering, will mean them meeting one day under a single tree – if that isn't lopped down to give the proposed HS2 super-railway a straight run from Brum to Crewe.

Smethwick illustrates the point. It's the birthplace of cricketer Sydney 'Barney' Barnes. A bowler who got very cross if he gifted boundaries is named in the hundredth edition of *Wisden Cricketers' Almanack* as one of its "Six Giants of the Wisden Century". What happened to his town, once called Smedeuuich, or 'settlement on the smooth land' – so perfect for cricket – can best be described as NUTS. There are still Staffies who, having been nowhere much during their lives are suddenly left scratching their noggins, after a bumpy ride.

When England won the footy World Cup in 1966 folk basking in the golden glow of the Jules Rimet Trophy stopped being on the ball. In the blink of an eye Smethwick was merged with the boroughs of Oldbury and Rowley Regis to form the new County Borough of Warley, which lock, stock and barrel got stuffed into Worcestershire. Then, five years before our kitchen mouse incident, Warley merged with West Bromwich, got labelled Sandwell Metropolitan Borough, and was plonked into a new county entity, West Midlands. Which solves my soggy Sandwell cricket query. Also severing its Staffs ties held since before the Domesday Book was Wolverhampton. Gobbling most of Bilston, Wednesfield and Tettenhall as well as smidgens of Sedgley, Coseley and Willenhall it became a West Midlands monster.

However, the can of worms needs a stroppy kick. West Midlands was born because of '72's Local Government Act. As well as removing Holland from Merseyside and conferring rights of appeal relating to the Home Counties (Music and Dancing) Licensing Act 1926, the act allowed Staffs, Worcestershire, and Warwickshire to be nibbled at. This is where 'NUTS' comes in. The word is an acronym for the mouthful: Nomenclature of Territorial Units for Statistics – a geocode standard for being nosy. A standard developed and regulated by the European Union landed West Midlands with the code UKG3 and Staffs UKG2. The point is to reference the subdivisions of countries for statistical purposes. Bureaucracy Brussels sprouted, really.

Perhaps, with hindsight, though, it was best Staffs did wash its hands of Smethwick.

From 1926 to 1931, Sir Oswald Mosley, the future founder of the British Union of Fascists was the Labour MP. Crank forward fourteen years to the General Election on 26 July 1945. The Labour MP voted in was Alfred Dobbs. However, the unfortunate soul was killed in a car crash within twenty-four hours, making him shortest-serving MP in this Island's history, if one turns a blind eye to a few cases of bods being plumped for posthumously.

Fast track to the 1964 General Election. While Harold Wilson's Labour grabbed Blighty from the Tories, a Tory snaffled Smethwick from Labour. Shadow Foreign Secretary Gordon Walker lost his seat in emotive fashion to Peter Griffiths, a chap who made dastardly use of the hot topic 'Immigration'. Had been so since the economic and industrial growth years after the Second World War when Sikhs from the Punjab in turbaned numbers chose Smethwick for a new life. They were invited. It was high on the Labour policy list that peoples from the Commonwealth could pitch up for work. Griffiths' campaign damned the notion. He pointed to 1962's race riots. And the word on the street was that his supporters slyly bandied about the slogan: "If you want a nigger for a neighbour, vote Liberal or Labour." Thoroughly unpleasant stuff.

And things got worse. In the second week of 1965 Smethwick had a visit from Malcolm X, the famed black activist from the US. Nine days before his assassination he fuelled further polemic when he told the press:

"I have come here because I am disturbed by reports that coloured people in Smethwick are being treated badly. I have heard they are being treated as the Jews under Hitler. I would not wait for the fascist element in Smethwick to erect gas ovens." It was impolitic as a rodent's squeak.

"You're descended from Parsley," Dad puffed through his thick greying moustache as we shove-tugging in tandem at sideboard resistance.

It was slightly better than being called a weed, but nevertheless I must have looked miffed. Dad sighed. "Let's leave this wretched brute for a minute." And for a while longer than that, we did. Allowing sweat-damp armpits time to dry Dad began a history lesson about the family tree, pruned for relevance and my attention span.

"Up north in Oswaldtwistle … it's near Accrington – Accrington Stanley? Football? … Robert Peel was born in the early 1720s. He was a farmer's son who grew up tall and robust wanting nothing to do with barren soil or thin animals. Instead he laid the family fortunes by shaking-up calico printing."

"Calico?"

"Heaven's sake, lad, it's a type of cotton cloth." Dad was back on comfortable ground. "It was used for drapes, bed covers, dresses. Feminine sort of

stuff. In those days the printing of calico was almost an unknown art."
"Shall try giving this lump another shove?"
"No. Just listen. Robert came up with a pretty pattern to print on the
calico: a sprig of parsley. And I've discovered how. He ate his supper off
pewter plates. For a bit of inventive fun one evening to amuse his daughter
Nancy he etched his plate with a parsley sprig.
"Vandal."
"Shh. 'What impression would I get from it in reverse if printed with
colour on calico?' your shrewd and sagacious ancestor thought."
I do remember yawning.
"Switch on and you'll be enlightened. A decrepit woman, Mrs Milton,
lived in one of the farm cottages. She kept a calendering machine, something
with rollers that presses cloth, smoothing it. So off goes Robert and squashes
the plate flat with an iron, rubs the etched leaf with some colour or other, and
bungs the plate and a piece of cotton rag through the old biddy's machine.
The impression made on the rag was quite passable. Robert decided he'd
invented roller printing on calico and ran with it to the point of ending up
with twenty-three factories. Several were in Burton-on-Trent."
"In Staffs?"
"Yep, definitely in Staffs. 'Nancy's pattern', as he called it, became
Robert's trademark and got produced ad infinitum – fashionable from
Launceston to Leith. Day in, day out, men and women put on their sparking
clogs and wearied to work to make it. Think of Lowry's chimneys, cobbles,
bricks and his matchstick figures. Lowry did something a lot of people can't
do. He found beauty in gritty smoke and industrial grime. Never know, you
might find similarities between Salford and Stoke. Anyway, Nancy's pattern
earned Robert the nickname 'Parsley' Peel, and he told everyone 'a man,
barring accidents, might be whatever he chose'."
"Herbidacious!" I said and broke into song. "I'm a very friendly lion
called Parsley, with a tail for doing jobs of every kind." It was my best imitation of Gordon Rollings' voice. There are some TV influences that are harder
to shift than a sideboard. And *The Herbs* on children's BBC was embedded.
But where Dad's ramble was leading left me with wilting interest. However,
I soon perked up.
"Parsley *Peel* had eight offspring. On his death his estate was split equally
between them and each, in today's money, became a millionaire."
"Oooh."
"Hmmm … Well as I say, a lot of the bunch moved to Staffordshire."
"Hm-hm."
"One became Prime Minister. You know about him, surely? Robert Peel,
First Baronet? *Sir* Robert? Founder of the police force? Bane of Ireland?"
I eagerly nodded knowledge.
"Wasn't in our direct line, mind you. Half-cousins, I'm afraid. Just as well.
Sir Robert's line got thicker. By all account his grandson was useless. A

gambler. A bad writer. A buffoon. You wouldn't want to tread in those foot-steps, would you?

"Nn-nn."

But a fine naval fellow who's in your mother's line married into cheese and a bloody great mansion." This titbit had my fervid attention and caused even a scuffle in the wainscot. "And…" There was a pregnant pause. "… your great-grandfather was a 'scholar at home'. Think of that, boy, when you pitch up at Keele minding your own politics."

"Absolutely." It wasn't as if I as about to do a tummy-tuck and drop completely into the unknown. I had absorbed an *independent*, in-depth fore-warning.

"You'll appear Gulliver-tall in the Potteries," pronounced Joe, an ex-Leek FE college lecturer. Joe Hoffman – Austrian, history buff, pub-snug lover, and general good-egg – had assessed my five-foot nine-inch frame through a glass-bottomed pewter pint tankard of drained bitter.

"North Staffordshire has up and downs. It's hilly, red brick, ale country," he counselled knowledgably. "Has a generous mix of … coalmines and iron-works. A hundred years ago the area was as isolated and self-sufficient. Aeons fashioned dialect and moulded a hobbit-like breed. At a pinch, some ten inches shorter than in fresh air places. Coal-grubby folk. Or clay dust white. Often disfigured. Often enfeebled. Silicosis and lead poisoning were … bummers. Others, the kiln-fire gazers, suffered red, watery-eyes."

Like the effect horses had on me, I thought.

"In hard-nosed conditions the hard-boiled Potters existed in fetid and crammed two-ups and two-downs. The backs had smelly privies across the yard. The fronts opened onto … um … malodorous pavements in narrow alleys. Course, as folk, they weren't the lowest of the low. They possessed hereditary skills. On the whole, they became a clearly marked social bracket. Beneath them, of course, were the usual hoi polloi – immigrant Welsh and Irish labourers. Above were the teachers, small shopkeepers, and clerks. Way above were the architects, doctors, solicitors, bankers, and … businessmen.

Pertinent for you, those at the top of the local tree included the infamous Sneyds. They owned Keele Hall, which is going to be looming over your new life. Stroll through 'Fresher's Gate' and you're in its cobbled yard."

I couldn't wait to discover whether Joe slurred the truth as copper and burnished gold leaves tumbled.

Learning Prudence

*"Affairs are easier of entrance than of exit; and it is but
common prudence to see our way out before we venture in."*
Aesop.

The 'Original Mirrors', in their black leather jackets and Doc Martens, the finest band of the 1980s in my humble opinion, got away taking their amazing music into nowhere before the border was manned. Frontman Ian Broudie's appropriate lyrics "Reflections of the way we used to be" continued to resonate.

The pack of young conservatives tenaciously holding onto the old ways flew Union Jacks and sang 'Jerusalem'. Ska saxophone and trumpet music bled from Wild John's curtain-drawn window. From others Bruce Springsteen battled Warren Zevon. The Ramones 'gabba-gabba hey' siphoned through. Punk was here and there. Pogoing and spitting along to The Clash's 'Spanish Bombs' was definitely there. We were almost cultivated.

The rugby club's helpful suggestion to strip-search and frisk "dangerous female students" soberly dismissed in a flash, the TV cameras had gone home for the night. The Free Republic of Keele's passport control and customs checkpoint volunteers had abandoned their small blue tent for a bop in the ballroom to 'I Only Want to Be With You'. It was good thinking not to stop 'The Tourists.'

Aptly named, the five who had first grouped together in Sunderland were the evening's booked band. Their names were all over NME. Peet Combes songwriter and guitarist; Dave Stewart, guitar; his girlfriend, Annie Lennox, on vocals and the occasional keyboards; Eddie Chin plucking bass, and Jim

Toomey beating grooves and drags on drums.

With the iron black spiral staircase from dressing room to ballroom stage a chuffing hazard, they were tipped to stay reasonably sober and off any dope-induced befuddlement before descending. Surprise then that Annie's squawk made even those at the back wince. "You nearly didn't have a band tonight!" she shrieked into the microphone. I noticed her very high heels.

Forty-five minutes later, bopped out and sweaty, revolutionaries repaired to the bar to down a third or fourth 'skiff' – a moniker for a plastic pint pot that kept the cheap keg beer warm, confused a quaffer whether the beer was cloudy or the pot scratched, and for weeks retained an aniseed taste after a Pernod promotion.

Amidst the bar hubbub friends Ejaz, Mark, and Rodge debated how to tweak chicken cooked in strawberry yoghurt. Ejaz's prototype had been yuk. Anna and Dyta talked dog care. While, immersed in Izaak Walton's *The Compleat Angler*, Anthony knocked ash from his pretentious pipe onto a Criminal Law textbook. Excusing myself I headed out for pud, chips, and curried gravy.

This meant steering passed the concourse post box where a couple of official letters had been sent. The first, addressed to the 'Prime Minster of Great Britain', cited John Locke's 'Second Treatise on Government' and declared independence. The other, to the 'International Olympic Committee', was a bid to host the next games. This was a touch premature. No one had thought of investing in anything bigger than an inflatable paddling pool given the weather being so ruddy 'nesh'.

A gale allied itself to whipped sheets of sogging rain. Hunkered into an unfashionable collar-up corduroy jacket patiently waiting, swaying like the ceiling-high skiff column, which wasn't all my own work, I focused on Toby pegging it across campus, land once gifted to the mediaeval crusading order the Knights Templar by King Henry II.

"Rufus! RUFUS! GERROFF!"

Toby's beer-lapping golden retriever, the wind in its ears, had again decided to lollop aboard the day's last bus out into England and foreign clay.

Hands on knees and gasping unchivalrous swear words into his beard Toby had to believe the dog would be fine. Previous occasions had seen much tail-wagging at journey's end at the city centre bus station. Boasting ironic Moorish precast concrete arches, it was a contender for grimmest building in the Midlands and not a place any human would want to go after dark unless out of necessity. Complaints varied, from dirty, depressing, uninviting and intimidating, to being windy, which sometimes correlated with lack of toilet facilities.

A cyclist just visible by a beam from a fading battery shouted three words at a gaggle saluting both the bus's passing and Toby's thumbed-down rattling Rover. The first two words were: "you Commie." The third I'm too polite to repeat.

The saluters broke into singing the Free Republic's National Anthem to the tune of *You'll Never Walk Alone*. "…No cuts! No Cuts! / Until they are stopped, / We'll govern on our own / We'll govern on our own." All in good jest but having a serious message. Mrs Thatcher's severe cuts to Higher Education budgets promised damaging effects on universities and their students. "Peanuts for education leads to banana republic creation – UDI at Keele," proclaimed a press release. "NO CUTS," screamed the water soluble white paint riskily daubed on the chapel roof.

This was the 'Kremlin on the Hill'. Had been, for that matter, since the early '60s.

Personally, I don't think the University's first Principal, Lord A. D. 'Sandie' Lindsay of Birker, quite had this in mind when commenting to two crest-fallen, squelchy socked professors attending their job interviews, "Yes, but you must see it with the eye of imagination…."

Albeit that the ballroom dome inflated an architect's pride, the hub of rebellion – the concrete and glass whole of the students' union – was getting a rinsing. Likened to a Mississippi steamboat, the building had its foundation stone laid way back in 1961 by HM the Queen in the presence of HRH the Princess Margaret, the University's Chancellor. Which is to say she was its honorary head. The event perhaps gave cause for the royal sisters to later become slightly rueful.

However, it wasn't they who had the vision. It was the Lindsay and his politically-minded vicar friend Thomas Horwood, the Rector of Etruria, a Stoke-on-Trent suburb named after the district in Italy putting itself on the map through the artistic products of Etruscan folk. Quite right then that Josiah Wedgwood should choose the Potteries version for his neo-classical Etruria Hall.

Josiah and especially his son Josiah II and his family split their time between the hall and their other base, Maer Hall, 5 or so miles south of Keele, where Josiah II would often invite his nephew Charles Darwin to stay. Made sense. Charles' mum was a Wedgwood. And not only did Charles grub around for Maer earthworms that became the origin of his *Origin of Species*, he also successfully proposed to his cousin Emma Wedgwood in the library once he returned from those five years aboard HMS *Beagle* – a journey Charles was part of only because Uncle Josiah persuaded Charles' dad to let him go.

Safe to say, Keele was Lindsay and Horwood's tremendous experiment. And there was help from another quarter: Barnett Stross. He should be acknowledged as another of the co-founders. A medical doctor and political firecracker he amassed a beloved art collection that was donated to the university. Lowry's 'The Mill Gates' and Alston Emerson F. Emery's 'Longton

Ovens' are among paintings by likes of Shi-he Dai, Julie Held, and Rowley Smart. On Valentine's Day 1964 Stross received a knighthood for services to The Arts. But more about him later.

Post-war the country was economically spent. Society was falling apart. Had been since the Great War, the Great Depression, and Germany's jack-boot-triggering World War Two. Highbrow mortals failing to powwow amongst themselves was not at all helpful. Lindsay adopted the mantra: "The man who only knows more and more about less and less is becoming a public danger."

Adamant that education was the key to recovery Lindsay was driven by what he saw as a needy local community that was dear to his heart.

His affection arose through a class of the Workers Educational Association founded in Longton. Supported by Oxford University's Balliol College, summer schools were held there and Lindsay was among the young tutors. The connection was made. A "people's university", Lindsay's expression, was a possibility.

And believing a Potteries-nucleus of learning could help change the world, Reverend Horwood stepped forward to add clout. Becoming leader of the Labour group on the Stoke City Council held the mantle of political fixer. The course he steered to create the university was both relentless and imaginative. And the nucleus of his attention was Keele Hall, a huge stone-pile the Sneyd family hadn't actually bust a gut to earn. Thanks to luck they made a handsome living from the rights to acres and acres of coal beneath their land.

Horwood targeted the hall's absent owner Colonel 'Sporting Ralph' Sneyd. How he persuaded him to the hand the creaky edifice over to academia is a story in itself.

"Sporting Ralph" kept his moustache trim and lived the privileged existence befitting a gentleman: a world tour, a spanking new yacht, fishing rods, shooting-parties with the King, three wives – glossing over one unpleasantly expensive divorce – and, costing a damned sight more: horse-racing. The 10 March, 1898 issue of *Vanity Fair* caricatured him in tweed togs, a thoroughbred horse breeder. The comic swipe was a follow on from Ralph building breeding stables at Keele Park. However, both they and the appended racecourse were defunct within a decade. A decline, some say, exacerbated by one of Ralph's houseguests.

In the same year as Ralph appeared in *Vanity Fair*, the raunchiest verse ever to arrive in print was published by a penniless poet under the pen name George Archibald Bishop. Ralph, perhaps craving a fruity buzz, sent an invite. It was accepted.

The bawdy rhymer was the infamous occultist Aleister Crowley, a Cambridge-educated chap of overbearing personality with both a liking to climb mountains and many epithets. 'The Great Beast 666' sticks out amongst other tongue-in-cheek apocalyptic titles he gave himself. He opined, "Modern morality and manners suppress all natural instincts, keep people ignorant of the facts of nature and make them fighting drunk on bogey tales." In polite society Crowley was very much "He-Who-Must-Not-Be-Named" with the British press dubbing him: "The Wickedest Man in the World". Although it seems Ralph, initially, didn't give a fig. He might have done in due course.

Gossip about magical jiggery-pokery at Keele Hall went viral. Especially as Crowley deciding Keele straddled paranormal ley lines and harboured a supernatural presence in its catacombs. A guard was needed. To fit the bill Crowley created an Egregore. Or so he said. Not in the dictionary, it's an occult thing – an autonomous psychic entity or 'thoughtform' capable of influencing a group of people. And to cover his bases, Crowley wandered around the estate scratching satanic symbols into trees. And if his feet had got muddy, a certain dragon-like bronze boot scraper wrought in the Apedale Valley awaited by the front door.

Herbert.

The stuff of heebie-jeebies, it explains why punters no longer wanted to come to Keele Park races. In 1901, and without hint of return, Ralph packed his bags.

Up for rent, the monstrous hall sprawled heavy on the earth soon had tenants. They weren't locals. Grand Duke Michael Mikhailovich of Russia, the Tsar's black sheep cousin, and his new wife Countess Sophie von Merenberg moved in. Ten years previously Sophie was smitten after Michael saved her from the back of ... a runaway horse. The Grand Duke knew it was pointless asking for the necessary marriage permission. Sophie's maternal grandfather was the famous poet-author Alexander Pushkin and through him, she had black African ancestry. The Tsar stripped Michael of his military titles and exiled him from Russia for marrying below his station. Keele Cricket Club, however, saw a mighty benefit from the palaver. Out of the blue it had a Russian moneybags patron. And things didn't end there. Playing the surrogate English country squire, the Grand Duke became the heart and soul of the local community and on one occasion fêted King Edward VII.

Meanwhile, Ralph's racecourse pushed up daisies and later had its home straight buried under M6 asphalt. Uttoxeter, however, arose as a phoenix-like substitute. A company formed to take over Ralph's racecourse licence and interests proved a dab hand at organising galloping gee-gees and gamblers.

As for Ralph, with spells on the Staffordshire hill having taken on different meaning, he converted his Keele stables into his private lodgings. Visits were rare, though. Instead he preferred Claridge's in London until the Great War brought him a moment of historical destiny. Posted to Paris as a Deputy Assistant Provost Marshal – a military police role – he arrested Dutch-born Margaretha Zelle, better known as Mata Hari. The notorious exotic dancer and courtesan, trumpeted as being a German spy, was accused of counterespionage. Namely, she revealed secrets that resulted in the deaths of at least fifty thousand men, almost the capacity of Stoke City's old Victoria Ground.

Margaretha's trial proved controversial. Her lawyer was unable to cross-examine any of the witnesses. Found guilty, she was put before a dawn firing squad of twelve French Zouaves on 15 October 1917. She was forty-one, wore a heavy silk kimono over her nightdress, and was neither bound nor blindfolded. Sporting Ralph can't have felt too proud.

And he turned up his nose and stubbornly refused to part with his distant, shabby hall for all Reverend Horwood's attempts at flattery and chequebook waggling. But the hall had taken a battering having been wartime requisitioned for British and American troops waiting to be sent to Normandy after D-Day and then becoming a refugee camp, had. Horwood wasn't for giving up but timing had to be of the essence. And in 1948, after the unsolved murder of a Polish woman slaughtered on her way back to camp after a Newcastle-under-Lyme party got brushed under the carpet, it was.

Horwood shoved a pen into Ralph hand when, distracted, he was tuned into a horse race radio commentary. In a state of euphoria because of his nag won Ralph signed the away his ancestral home. The Egregore's powers had markedly waned.

The purchase got Lindsay's dream moving. Keele, in its early guise as the University College of North Staffordshire, opened for lectures in 1949. There was now a place where essential specialist and expert knowledge could be balanced with "a wide outlook and general understanding." And being aware of a shared European cultural heritage, a balance would hopefully keep threats of rotten science and unethical political systems in check.

To sum his aspirations up before the Grim Reaper swung his scythe Lindsay said: "If we are going to try and keep a democratic country and maintain understanding of one another, we have to send out people from our universities who can do the technical stuff and who at the same time have an understanding of political and social problems and of the values that lie behind them."

Keele set out to achieve this vision, beginning with conquering social problems. By 1966, 'bum-freezers', the traditional academic gowns, were only discoverable by torchlight mouldering in Keele's curiously spooky cobwebbed tunnels. The future was to be 'hip'. The label 'Brain Bunnies' was bestowed on a group of female students frolicking beside the campus' murky ornamental lakes. Photographed to stun they popped up in a "latest fashions" feature in the groovy *Honey* magazine. Amongst them was Marina Lewycka, little guessing one day she'd be short-listed for the Orange Prize with her bestseller *A Short History of Tractors in Ukrainian*. A university sweatshirt was introduced, the first of its kind in Britain, although really cool students tended to bundle to Longton's Kinki Klothes for swirly skirts, tab collars, and polka dots.

Come 1969, Keele, quicker on the buzzers than Jesus College, Cambridge and congratulated by question master Bamber Gasgoigne on winning University Challenge, was being described as "the most original innovation in British university education in the twentieth century". Oh, it absolutely was.

One merely has turn the calendar to a year later when, on 28 October, a cry went up that wouldn't have gone amiss at Hogwarts. "Let humming levitate the Vice Chancellor's house!"

A Radio Stoke volunteer, Gerry Northam, captured 'live' what followed on a portable reel-to-reel Uher tape deck. The aims stated by Pete, the student spokesperson, were twofold: to achieve a 'spiritual unity' amongst the gathered throng of about three hundred and to raise the pretty red-brick residence attached to its tiny clock tower, formerly Sporting Ralph's breeding stables, two hundred and fifty feet in the air. Vice Chancellor Willie Campbell-Stewart could look forward to a grand panorama over the top of a beautiful chestnut avenue to the M6 motorway. Tut-tut.

It was a blatant act of plagiarism.

A similar incident had occurred in USA when a group circled the White House to try levitating that. Part of the anti-Vietnam protests, it was reported. The Keele effort was more mundane – a wheeze from the drama society. And before anything moved Willie's wife, Ella, bustled out the front door to politely ask, "what on earth was going on". Pete explained. She listened dutifully and after some thought said, "Alright dear, but please put it back when you've finished with it."

Like the White House effort, levitating proved unsuccessful – managing only to raise the building "about six feet, give or take six feet." The excuse was feeble: not enough students joining hands to completely encircle the building. For Gerry, though, the shenanigans proved the cornerstone of his BBC career.

Willie didn't get off lightly. He had mighty student demos to cope with. They were over his persistent refusal to allow students to see their own files. Psychological warfare had to be resorted to disperse a particularly troublesome rally. A porter loudly reminded the protesters that *Dr Who* was about to start on television. Then there were the naked students in the middle of the roundabout and the burning of the prefab administration huts. Both proved impotent. Things would have been so different had there been a Data Protection Act and the Freedom of Information Act. Yet, throughout, Willie's unruffled tact and good sense ensured that the university's business of teaching and examining continued uninterrupted despite the dire publicity.

All in all, not bad for goings-on around and inside a once dilapidated old house near an obscure village where happily the electric was still on. Fingers crossed it would remain so. Rumours were abroad that the local power station had been ordered to renege on its 'no cuts' pre-independence agreement.

Over my feet blew the daily bulletin sheet bearing its new calendar: 'Day 3'. That's to say, the period since the start of UDI, or to stretch it out, Unilateral Declaration of Independence. Seventy-two hours since North Staffs Poly made claim to be Staffordshire's premier seat of higher education.

Keele's newishly appointed Vice Chancellor, Professor David Harrison, had to grin a bear it. And bear it he did. The honorary life member of the student union remarked in a calm, gravelly voice with a strong Potteries accent, "'e's a very nice man." Said emphatically, and as if there was a D in the middle of "very", the words were those of the stout and jovial Neil Baldwin. A marvellous fellow.

Asked if he actually knew Professor Harrison, Neil replied "I've just had tea with him and his wife." And there lies the rub. Given Neil's fancy to don a clerical collar the Vice Chancellor may have been under the impression that he was Keele's Anglican chaplain.

Neil enriched lives. Fact. Wandering up from Newcastle-under-Lyme in 1960 he sauntered into the students' union, an engaging schoolboy with learning difficulties, and became a fixture. His connection was purely informal. He never worked at Keele in any capacity. Yet a cornered fresher, I signed up for his Neil Baldwin Football Club, of which he was the manager, captain, and the every year winner of Player of the Year.

Other genuine tales about Neil are two-a-penny. He once sold a Keele rag magazine to Prime Minister Harold Wilson and buttonholed the Duke of Edinburgh for a chat about world problems. Regrettably, Neil wasn't available to help with the mess in front me in the chip van queue.

Liz, a face I knew, squeaked. Brown sauce had added itself to her striped uni scarf colours of black pudding, tomato and egg, furthering her bad mood that had begun with the afternoon's highlight.

A driver following his bonnet into the Free Republic, seeing the checkpoint had reversed out pronto before nosing forward sloth-slow. A quizzical 'guard' lowered a black-painted AK47 water sprayer and went to chat. The chap behind the wheel revealed himself as a serving member of the armed forces recently returned from a Northern Ireland tour. The checkpoint manned by 'paramilitaries' had seemed a tad too kosher.

"For certain there'll be cuts if news gets out," whined Liz "Terminal ones. Dad'll stop my allowance. His friends are needling him, saying: 'Bad luck your daughter's at Keele.' Ten minutes ago on the phone he demanded I leave here 'right now', work a gap year, and apply to go somewhere less radical. Told him I'm not going anywhere."

Having had a similar telephone conversation not long before her, I jiggled my loose change. "Mine also says he'll keelhaul me if I cause any trouble."

"What? Confined to Keele Hall? That's awful."

Rather than argue the point I chose to accept the pity. Anyway, to suggest I queued import dependent on haute cuisine was true. The chip van proffering a 'cure-all' was plunked in the loftiest altitude university car park west of Siberia. My throat's notional ale marker was submerged. I thought it best to have something to soak up any threat from the point of no return. And, as local leafy greens were only found autumnally on the adjacent golf course, I was a tad bunged up. Just a gut feeling, then, that I was fitting into Potteries' life.

Past letters on this subject were stashed in the university library. Amongst them is one written on Thursday 2 December 1909. Arnold Bennett, Staffs famous novelist, whose name has become less associated with books like *The Grim Smile of The Five Towns* than with a fish-filled omelette, was the J.K. Rowling of his day. Sitting at his mum's table at 179 Waterloo Road, Burslem he penned a bleak missive to his wife Marguérite. "…It is barbaric – thick rain and furious wind … I am still constipated!!! If I don't go within half an hour I shall shoot it out with my revolver."

Not even having access to a little water pistol I placed my foodie order. To quote dear old Arnie, again: "Good taste is better than bad taste, but bad taste is better than no taste."

"Cummin up, duck." Sal, the round-faced lady in the fat-stained pinny wiped a hand through grease-lank hair and smiled beatifically. A slippery suet pastry encasing gristly morsels of steak and scraps of pig's kidney in gunky gravy got baptised from a ladle. Meantime hubby, Bill, baled pale chips out their broiling oil bath.

"Can I have a bit *more* gravy on my pud?"

"Course, shug." Sal obliged with her ladle. How sweet, I thought, having mastered that 'shug' was short for sugar, a term of endearment when closing a sentence, as in 'Ta, shug'. 'Duck', on the other hand, is a greeting derived from the Saxon word 'ducas', and plied to show respect. Both 'duck' and 'shug' are part of Potters culture and along with 'love' are said to everyone, very much to add a personal touch.

Bolstered by affection I had a further question for the chip van lady. "The city centre bus station? Is it in Hanley or in Hanley Duck?"

"It's just Hanley, duck. There's no Hanley Duck, shug." With that she stuck a wooden fork in the drowned suet.

A small, gangly dog nuzzled my jeans. Jem. Shorthaired and mongrel, her ancestry leaned towards the dark side of whippet and Jack Russell. Tugging on the leash was Anna. A Sheffield miner's daughter she felt at home with scenic Silverdale Colliery below the hill brow. "It's out of hand," she said.

"What is?"

"Keele's republic. Just heard Kurt Waldheim's coming to pay us a visit. Pinch a chip?"

Waldheim, Secretary-General of the United Nations, at Keele? I wondered if the there had been a misspelling in his diary. Students enjoy the jape that the University's named after the motorway service station. But in broader conversation Keele can sometimes be confused with Kiel, the place where Marina Lewycka was born in a refugee camp. Its university is the largest, oldest, and most prestigious in the German state of Schleswig-Holstein. Once it was even the second largest uni in Denmark, too. Thing is, although the pronunciation is the same, Kiel was established in 1685.

Kurt was Austrian with a shady Nazi past. Indeed, the *Guardian* reported on his appointment: "the flak received from abroad was a huge setback in the international development of a country which, after 1945, had successfully managed to develop a cosy image built around Mozart and mountain yodellers".

In turn, Kurt was quoted as saying, "I wasted years worrying about what other people thought".

"Daft Valdy having any association with us on his CV," I said, giving Jem a stroke.

And I held on to that reckoning, until I witnessed a brown Rolls Royce purr towards a smartly dressed welcoming committee gathered outside Keele Hall. Coincidental or not, Cuba had recognised the Free Republic's UDI. Yet an armoured personnel carrier rolling tracks through campus was a surprise. A sound enough reason for me to experiment upon Marguérite's missive to AB from Italy in 1921 emphatic that, "Frascati's good red wine is a laxative".

Course I compromised, filling a skiff with affordable tannin-infused red vinegar, determined to relax my sphincter while going easy on the curried gravy until Keele returned to being part of the United Kingdom. Happily it did shortly afterwards. Not, however, before a child was born in the Republic.

Imagine the fun answering to bureaucracy in later life.

"Nationality?"

" Keelite." And then produce the passport.

Surprisingly, despite the mischief of UDI, only a single lecture got cancelled. And that happened to be knee-jerk. The cause lay in New York. John Lennon had been shot dead. Our Liverpudlian lecturer, found bumparked on his table, legs swinging, was unable to focus on swotty trivialities.

The time was ripe to do a Ralph Sneyd and escape the hill – a scene change that would have me flicking a rag to keep coal dust off my Original Mirrors LP. For his part, Neil Baldwin would begin his life adventure. Leaving his Thistleberry home in Newcastle-under-Lyme, he became Nello the Clown travelling in Sir Robert Fossett's circus.

Rhino, Peel and Chips

"The fossil record is incredible when it preserves things, but it's not a complete record."
Jack Horner, palaeontologist.

For three months of the year the Staffordshire sun can't be arsed to rise. At best it musters a cold glow behind a low-hanging fog that hides the top of the Pye Green BT Tower. And by mid afternoon it goes somewhere else.

So a Saharan-style desert with huge rolling sand dunes doesn't quite fit Staffordshire's description as "the dark bit in the back of England's cupboard".

Nor, quite, do river deltas and the swampy shallows of a tropical sea.

And let's be frank, any local crocodile cruising a coral reef passed trilobites, or a dumpy cacops – the ancestor of frog and toad – having a waddle in a humid, dense Carboniferous forest, were clueless about the possibilities of potters' clay and miners' coal seams three hundred million years ago.

The warmth-loving flora and fauna, though, had long gone when the time clock is whanged forward to forty-two thousand years BC – a precise point in history when fickle nature turned Staffordshire into Arctic tundra. Grass and herbs fed the likes of woolly mammoths, reindeer, bison, and, charmingly, horses. Wolves and hyenas prowled. And there were beetles that today are only found in northern Siberia or the high plateaux of central Asia.

So heck, yes it was mighty cold. An anciently horny beast without extant local relatives categorically proved it. Found well preserved in Whitemoor Haye quarry close to Alrewas, was one of Britain's most significant fossil finds in the last hundred years.

Irrefutably, the woolly rhino was a biggie – a creature in its prime, plant remains still stuck between its teeth. Researchers reckoned the critter met a rapid end after becoming stuck in quicksand while chomping at the edge of a water channel. Or, then again, cut off on part of a floodplain, it drowned. Logical. Alrewas gives the hint. The Anglo-Saxon of it is Alor-wæsse. Meaning 'alluvial land growing with alder trees'.

Nowadays, tree species are multifarious, due in no small part to the National Memorial Arboretum – a spiritually uplifting place, still in its teens and where poppies grow, "which honours the fallen, recognises service and sacrifice, and fosters pride in our country". Here tree numbers exceed fifty thousand, spread over a hundred and fifty acres.

Be that as it may, Professor Danielle Schreve laid her red and white measuring rod beside the heavy-skulled skeletal jigsaw on the sandstone hump and took a photo. Presenting hard evidence of very non-tropical ice age chills, great gratitude was felt towards the old stick-in-the-mud.

A term that was equally smack-on for singular coves in my maternal family, like my Lichfield-born great-grandad Lionel Peel who became a Shenstone 'Scholar at Home' harbouring a love of sausages. Breezing over a lunatic's shotgun massacre in 1929 that left house walls "bespattered with blood and brains", the most notable event in his village's history came in 1943 when Mrs Lucy Sutton celebrated her hundred and first birthday. She "still weeds her own garden", reported the *Lichfield Mercury* about a life spent "cutting mangolds and spreading manure on the fields".

I though headed for Drayton Bassett, in the extreme south-west corner of the county. A hundred years earlier than Lucy's great event, *The Illustrated London News* wrote of Prince Albert attending a shoot and having "killed sixty pheasants, twenty-five hares, eight rabbits and one woodcock." Not a bad day's bag. What interested me was where the fauna demised – Drayton Manor, the seat of my family's notorious branch.

Beginning at the Norman Conquest the estate had been through various noble hands. The Duke of Buckingham though had little say in letting go. Executed in 1483, his home was collared by the Crown who held on it for a while. However, 1666's Hearth Tax Assessment, as well noting Drayton's forty-two fireplaces, had the Duchess of Somerset down as owner. The soot and smut though must have been too much for her because later the Earl of Leicester is found selling the manor on to the Earl of Essex. In about 1790 the Earl palmed it off to the *nouveau riche*.

Ownership of Drayton passed from blue blood to the common red of Parsley Peel's son, the second Robert Peel. As first baronet, he began a further confusion of Roberts.

The Lancashire cotton manufacturer and calico printer had been living on his nerves. The industrial north a seditious hotbed Robert sought calm with cachet for his impressionable family.

Fitting the bill was unassuming Tamworth. In spitting distance of Drayton it had been England's original capital. This was the doing of Offa. The mighty King of Mercia and all England, he of the eighth century great dyke dissuading Welsh raiders, had his palace here. The southern wimps of Wessex and Anglia were firmly under Offa's control for a while, and he was on excellent terms with the Muslim world. Happy days.

But I'll wager Robert would had second thoughts about the Drayton move if seedy Tamworth news was anything like 2015's. Snapped in broad daylight in Gorsey Bank Road to make the tabloids was a mum-of-four, her leggings round her ankles. Behind was her toy-boy half-naked – the bottom half. He offered exegesis: "We both have fish tanks with me keeping piranhas and her a couple of turtles and we were on our way to look at the garden centre fish section... I said to her 'Fancy a quickie?' and obviously she did." Neither appeared the least bit sheepish.

Honestly, I'm no prude. Not since getting down close and intimate birthing lambs in straw-strewn barns, any rate. Pulling on forelegs and wiping mucus-slimed noses is closure of a natural process begun when the ram tupped the ewe in some degree of privacy. Heaven knows where the pair of fishy Tammies getting the horn and bonking in a modern glass-sided telephone box might lead.

A high street newsagent was definitely disillusioned by the unsavoury goings on. "Tamworth," she sighed handing me the change for the latest copy of *Private Eye*, "is probably the only place in England you can see copulating, drinking, puking, fighting, bleeding, getting arrested, bowling, and … skiing, all within a ten minute walk." Skiing? Of course!

Tamworth has a habit of making eccentric business decisions. I recalled the Reliant Motor Car Company's 'hedgehog slayer' – the three-wheeler van. The bodies were once made in an outbuilding at the Plough Inn, about a quarter of a mile from the factory. Four men had to grab a corner each and manually lug the shell the whole way. Charmingly old school but hardly cutting edge industry. Now the town is all about being home to "the UK's first full-sized real-snow indoor ski slope" which sits oddly with a competitive streak aimed at 'Britain in Bloom'.

But best get back on track.

Before becoming Tamworth's MP, Robert the first baronet had made more than enough to afford stumping up the ackers for Drayton Manor. And after moving there his bank account climbed further into the black. At the confluence of the Birmingham and Fazeley and the Coventry canals, his new cloth mill at Fazeley Junction, in-between Tamworth and Drayton Bassett, but closest of all to Drayton Manor, began to flourish.

The mill, an impressive five-storey brick affair, looms over a low-arched bridge. From it I found myself ignored by a flotilla of nonchalant, drifting Canada geese negotiating the junction's tight turns. For a coal barge to have done so was always a lot more difficult. Black cargo got shed. In tough times local knowledge had children acquire old buckets. A few holes were punctured in them, bits of rope were attached, and the canal bottom dragged. This way heaps of free coal for cooking fires and hobs got collected.

The Peels used the junction to barge their cloth everywhere.

And to tie up a loose and confusing end, it was Robert Peel's lad – Robert the second baronet – who, having followed his dad into the Tamworth seat, had two cracks as Prime Minister – between 1834 and 1835 and again between 1841 and 1846.

He was the handsome chap that fathered the police force, paved the way for Catholic emancipation, and wrote the Tamworth Manifesto published in the national press, laying down the basic principles of the modern Conservative Party. The same Robert who, before helpfully repealing the Corn Laws, that in effect sacrificed his government, sent Prince Albert the invite to blast pheasants. Naturally, Queen Victoria had accompanied her hubby to the venue.

Arriving as house guests the royal couple were by all accounts delighted to find Drayton Manor transformed. Robert had done away with the creaky antiquated manor house and its triple-decker banqueting hall, and replaced it with a resplendent mansion ticked-off nicely by a three-storey tower. Not forgetting expansive stunningly landscaped grounds. Master architect Robert Smirke, known for his Greek revivalist style, had worked diverse magic, redesigning Drayton as mock Elizabethan.

Robert ensured the new grand rooms and galleries were elaborately dressed with costly furniture, expensive antiques, and a priceless art collection. The pièce de résistance, procured by Robert in 1823, being Rubens' 'Chapeau de Poil', a cleavage-showing lass wearing the portrait's subject, a wide-brimmed feather-festooned fur hat.

Hankering for a comparable portrait of his wife, Lady Julia, Robert employed the services of Sir Thomas Lawrence, an artist of flamboyant and virtuoso style by then in his twilight years. The finished picture, featuring Julia arrayed in a white fur-trimmed cloak and an elaborately plumed hat, was first exhibited at the Royal Academy in 1827. A critic claimed it to be among "the highest achievements of modern art."

Our good baronet was quite the talk of London town. And rightly so. He was sitting on a mint. His portfolio was gobsmacking: industrial and domestic properties, acres and acres of countryside, and clusters of urban Tamworth. Robert could satisfy himself being head of one of the country's richest families. But the happy condition was ephemeral.

A tumble from a horse occurred in 1850. The fault of a Constitution Hill mole ironically almost put Sir Robert deeper under the sod than itself. Entombment in the vault of the Drayton Barrett parish church, Robert's wish, was however granted. The church's internal and immense gothic memorial monument, his family's indulgence, cost a bomb. Robert's brother Edmund got nowt but a small vault all to himself beside the churchyard gate.

The mole incident, though, impacted further – inducing a fall of hugely greater magnitude. Within a couple of generations the house of Peel was unable to pay neither the local blacksmith, nor chimneysweep, nor iceman. Larger creditors lost bundles. It was an eye-watering drama that touched bookmakers, second-hand car sales, theatre dressing rooms, and the high-born of Europe; ending with a Japanese bomb.

Problems raised their ugly head when the Prime Minister's son, Robert the third baronet, wasn't up to scratch. Not by a long chalk. The brains, integrity, and self-esteem of his father or grandfather were AWOL. Instead, a peacockish and narky nature, combined with a rakish disposition and wasteful extravagance, set the path to rack and ruin.

Palmerston appointing him Irish Secretary in 1861 was definitely not a good pick. His words, often unwise and irrational, quickly opened him to ridicule. Crackpot letters dashed into print in the *Times* were right up there. One can only imagine what the Irish thought.

Still, he found love of sorts. On January 13, 1856, Peel married Lady Emily Hay, seventh daughter of George Hay, eighth Marquess of Tweeddale. They shared one passion – horse racing. It was to become a story akin to Keele's 'Sporting Ralph' Sneyd, but on a much, much grander scale.

Robert and Emily went at it full-throttle. Livestock was bought and raised. State-of-the-art-stables got built at Bonehill, a Fazeley parish. Horses were bred. A racecourse was laid out. Blue and gold racing silks were adopted. And for gambling purposes the third baronet chose the alias Mr F. Robinson. As good a name as any, I guess.

And, oh my, what lavish socialite champagne parties!

Fazeley became alive. Fashionable crowds cheered the Drayton Stakes and the Middleton Handicap. Alas, jockeys in the Peels' silks were a rarity in the winners' enclosure. Stubbornly, horseflesh expenses soared. And, properly acerbated by F. Robinson, money evaporated fast and furiously.

A Drayton Manor extension can't have helped. A grand aviary stuffed with exotic birds wasn't actually necessary but was part of the spendthrift whirl. Course, there was 'the season': the London town house, the Geneva villa, the flat on the Riviera, and the temptations of Monte Carlo.

Then came the new brainwave: Greyhound coursing. Unappreciated by hares chased down for a mauling, the sport had known as "the sport of queens" since Elizabeth the First established it in the sixteenth century. Only once a spectator, I felt the entertainment was worryingly barbaric while peering through mizzle and fog at excited men, careering hounds, and hearing leporids' screams. This was Liverpool's infamous Waterloo Cup, 'the blue ribbon of the leash'. An annual calendar event begun 1836, it vanished amid chunters in 2005 due to government's legislative stick.

Sidestepping all that, Robert became a frontrunner developing another avenue for a longdog's CV: Greyhound racing. There was some logic. While attracting the punters, woofers had cheaper overheads to nags. A flat cap was cheaper than a top hat so to speak. The rot thus truly set in. When Sir Robert went to the dogs. Everything else went too. He was in debt, big-time.

Creditors became litigious arriving at Drayton Manor with Sheriffs execution orders. Things had got heavy. Sir Robert was threatened with prison over refusing to account to the Charity Commissionaires while sole trustee of the Peel School Charity.

In March 1871, the Peel art collection of seventy-seven pictures, including 'Chapeau de Poil', and eighteen drawings, was sold to the National Gallery for £75,000. By 1884 the ten thousand acres of family estates were being broken up and sold off piecemeal. Lady Emily disposed of the stud farm but by now it was too late, the fortune had gone.

On May 9, 1895, Sir Robert died from a brain haemorrhage. Step forward young Sir Robert, fourth baronet. Let's call him Robert Four. A chip off his dad's block, he enjoyed a broad spectrum of popularity. A firm favourite with Fazeleyites he also fitted into the high-living clique that revolved around Queen Victoria's son Edward, Prince of Wales. Drayton Manor became a beguiling honeypot of pretty actresses, amongst them the famous Lily Langtry. Genteel hands would clap him at the cricket, played on the estate's deer park pitch.

He dabbled in writing and published two pretty bad novels, *A Bit Of A Fool* and *An Engagement*, and was always appearing in the gossip columns of the nationals. His romantic entanglements often got him into hassle. A duel with a fiery Italian over a lover was one of a litany of mini-sagas.

However, his dad's death cramped Robert Four's style. The estate trustees only allowed him £3000 a year. For the charming socialite with champagne tastes on beer money this was a devastating blow. His wine bill alone for one year was £1475. Best marry well, he thought.

Baroness Mercedes de Graffenreid seemed ideal. Oh dear. He believed her a wealthy heiress. She believed him a rich man with a title. And yes, the latter was authentic. The engagement was speedy. The wedding was a lavish entertainment. A torchlight procession welcomed the bride and groom to Drayton Manor. Mutual disappointment followed.

Within a year, the London Bankruptcy Court had Robert Four admitting liabilities that he was unable to meet. A spending curb might be imagined. Not a bit of it. A Swiss Lodge at the entrance of Drayton Manor was commissioned as a present for his wife. Perhaps to help keep her sweet, or just as likely to keep up appearances. Either way, it wasn't for long. He and Lady Peel did a runner to fashionable Paris. As the means to exist they nabbed a valuable heirloom: the portrait of Lady Julia.

Their sojourn was short. Robert Four was summoned back across the Channel to attend court.

The judge ordered that the picture should be restored to the estate and that no other items should be removed. Robert Four retorted that he had a perfectly good explanation for what he had done. He was simply offsetting debt by cash-raising. In return the judge mentioned the word 'prison'.

Drayton Manor was officially pillaged. Plate, engravings, linen, saddlery, clocks, statues, ornaments, and jewellery were loaded onto railway trucks London bound for auction – thimblefuls toward the well of debt. Although things were desperate Robert Four stubbornly maintained an expensive London social whirl.

The odd trip abroad managed him a stroke of luck. Reputedly, he was the man 'who broke the bank at Monte Carlo'. Which isn't quite as impressive as it sounds. Put simply, it's winning every chip on the table. Of course, debts gobbled Robert Four's winnings and continued to need hungry feeding.

Yet there was probably a tad of celebration, nevertheless. For, lo and behold, an heir was born. His name could only be … Robert. So best call him Bobby. As the world entered the twentieth century his mum vanished off to Switzerland for good. Left behind, the lad was at the mercy of Robert Four's deteriorating health and temper. This was whipped-up further by the family solicitor doing a bunk with a whacking amount of money. Robert Four felt the need to take out his ire on something or someone. Bobby was the easy target. The thrashings only stopped when his pater opted to spend life in 'the Smoke'.

For Bobby, existence was shared between Harrow and Fazeley Vicarage where the Reverend Melville Jones offered kindly sanctuary. However this didn't stop him absconding from school during the Great War. Desperately wanting to serve his country he gave a false age and joined the army. Discovered, he was hauled back in disgrace to continue maths equations and Latin homework.

'Down' from Cambridge, coming of age in 1919 saw the lad with guts begin to flourish. Drayton Manor estate employees, to whom he was clearly a legend, made Bobby party guest of honour. "Our Bobby" they called him.

Soon as possible he enlisted in the Coldstream Guards. Unfortunately suspected TB meant he was invalided out and he moseyed to Australia to recuperate.

After steeling himself Bobby did return to England where he tried to make a living selling used cars. Pleas from his pater, now bankrupt for the sixth time, to marry a wealthy woman to recoup the family fortune were flatly ignored. Bobby had found himself a convivial niche.

London, its old style music halls consigned to history's dustbin, was alive to new jazz music and smart reviews. The West End theatre scene immersed Bobby. Invites to fashionable parties filled his mantelpiece. He socialised regularly with Ivor Novello, Noel Coward, George Robey, Gladys Cooper, Gertrude Lawrence, and a charming young man, always incognito, known lovingly as David. There was no disguising that this was the Prince of Wales, later to become King Edward VIII – the king who later abdicated to marry the American love of his life, Wallis Simpson.

Catching Bobby's eye from across 'The Pond' was a tiny Canadian actress-cum-comedienne called Beatrice Lillie. A firm favourite with London audiences, she had risen to stardom in such shows as Andre Charlot's 'Bran Pie', 'Tabs', and 'Oh Boy'. She would solemnly parody the flowery performing style of earlier decades, mining such songs as 'There are Fairies at the Bottom of our Garden' for every double entendre, while other numbers showcased her exquisite sense of the absurd.

She gave the first public performance of Noel Coward's 'Mad Dogs and Englishmen'. And her comic matron routine 'One Double Dozen Double Damask Dinner Napkins' earned her the sobriquet of "Funniest Woman in the World". Bobby Peel fell head over heels and soon the gossip columns were full of their romance.

Come January 1920 and Fazeley was inundated with reporters from the national glossy mags and a galaxy of stars from the London stage. They had pitched-up for the wedding. Reverend Jones for one had never seen the like. He ensured his surplice was spotless, his dog-collar neat, and the flowers bedecking St Paul's church perfect.

Amongst the heaving pews of celebrity was a singular absentee. Bobby's pater was furious his son wasn't marrying an heiress.

In the autumn Lillie gave birth. Bobby had an heir. Robert would be the happy couple's only child.

The fourth baronet, meanwhile, went downhill fast. Giving up London for Drayton Manor, sick, sad, and paralysed from the waist down, veteran servants nursed him until his death in 1925, shortly after Tamworth gained an electricity supply.

Within a year or two Smirke's labour of love, marble columns and all, was levelled and sold for rubble – a fate unimaginable at the manor's lauded completion less than nine decades earlier. A fair bit of the demolition work was done by local miners earning a bob an hour – a bit of self-help during 1926's National Strike. As keepsakes, however, the clock tower was left lonely but intact and otters were allowed to remain undisturbed in the manor pool.

Bobby meanwhile moved into the Swiss Lodge and, inspired by Lillie, turned musical. He formed a dance band, 'Sir Robert Peel and the Bing Boys'. Robert on clarinet let it swing accompanied by saxophone, drums, double bass, and trumpet. Music halls across the country offered gigs. None, in his opinion, compared with playing at his own dance hall in the deer park cricket pavilion, the local social hub. The gamekeeper, a keen fan, had the habit of hiding his gun outside under a pile of leaves before attending … until the weapon got nicked. Nobody owned up. Stoats and foxes had a window of fun and crows could chuckle 'caw'.

Fair to say, cricket for Bobby was another love. He ran two cricket teams, over Saturdays and Sundays and hired two Warwickshire professionals.

And the halcyon days extended to football. Good Friday saw the Fazeley Association Football Cup contested. Teams arrived from the likes of Cannock and Nuneaton, and, as with the cricket, each team was allowed a professional duo. Each goal scored was reported by the release of a racing pigeon.

The Easter football, however, was cancelled in 1934 because of sudden news. Bobby was dead. "Peritonitis," the doctor said. "Bad bacteria in the blood," he explained. Everyone mourned. Two bricklaying brothers opened Edmund Peel's tomb for Bobby to be squeezed to rest inside. Hundreds gathered around the Drayton Bassett church for the funeral. Kids climbed up into the yew trees to get a superior view. A wreath shaped as cricket stumps, a bat and a ball was laid beside the coffin.

Easter eight years later and the tragedy compounded. HMS *Tenedos* was undergoing wartime repairs in Colombo Harbour on Easter Sunday, 5 April 1942, when it was bombed and sunk by Japanese aircraft. Thirteen naval lives were lost. Among them was Bobby and Lillie's son, ordinary seaman Sir Robert Peel, sixth baronet. He was twenty-two years old. Lillie never recovered.

To be sure to be sure, I checked the Fazeley War Memorial and found young Robert's name inscribed, as it should be. Nor had he been overlooked in Drayton Bassett church. Doubts assuaged I went to inspect the fate of the old estate right when the 110 Arriva Midlands bus disgorged a gaggle of excited passengers that headed towards Drayton Manor's drive – an infinitesimal percentage of well over a million thrill-seeking visitors a year.

I thought of Bobby. His beloved cricket pitch and dance hall had long gone. Ironically a greyhound stadium covered them over in the '40s, and the facilities became shared with speedway. In the '60s the stadium, in turn, made way for a housing estate. The rest of the Peel kingdom became Drayton Manor Theme Park and Zoo. Trendy meerkats have replaced the departed otters.

Where Prince Albert bagged his pheasants is Shockwave, Europe's only stand-up rollercoaster summarising the Peel saga nicely. And offset from the appropriate rides Maelstrom, Pandemonium, and Drunken Barrels is 'Bryan's slot machine museum'.

Gambler Robert Four must turn in his grave wondering why he never pondered a themed creation as the means for salvation. Instead, the Peel baronetcies had been obliterated – extinct as the woolly rhino.

Bull and Native Words

"Dialect words those terrible marks
of the beast to the truly genteel."
Thomas Hardy, writer and poet.

Following the red bonnet of Milami an aging but beautiful Fiat 500 I pootled over the bridge spanning the River Dove. "Welcome to the Creative County," read a sign. Whoopee, I'd briefly been to Derbyshire but was back for lunch and the company of a non-assiduous solicitor-cum-fisherman-cum-scatter-gun historian chum.

I landed on a pine bench in Tutbury, a village once producing alabaster, and I think I was allergic to the dog.

"We were lucky to find a table to perch at." Anthony stretched himself, loosened his red, white spotted, cravat, and sighed with contentment. Amazing, given he'd quit his pipe. "This used to be a sweet shop," he said.

Opened by Gary and Jane a couple of retirees, the 'Cask and Pottle' is one room. Staffordshire's first micro pub is also Anthony's favourite. We got served our pints of Dancing Duck straight from the cask. Our pork pies arrived magically from somewhere else.

On a wall were neatly painted ale measures. A 'pottle', I learned, was an archaic half-gallon – adequate enough for the tanker constitution. At the rear of the room, offering a view of the stillage was a window. Anthony craned his neck to stare thoughtfully through it. My book had been on his mind. "At least think about including standing stones. At very least the one stood in the Gun Hill heather commanding Jodrell Bank."

"Caterpillars," I said.

"Sorry?"

"The caterpillars of Gun Hill."

"You've lost me."

I told Anthony the story of how one morning, shortly after the outbreak of the Second World War, people living on and around Gun Hill opened their eyes to the surreal. Millions upon millions of caterpillars covered the ground, the hedges, the trees, and every other flora known. The locals convinced themselves that the caterpillars had been dropped by a German Zeppelin airship. The dastardly intention had been to destroy crops needed for the war effort, they said. A freak of nature was dismissed out of hand.

Anthony harumphed. "Burial mounds are vital, too. You have to include burial mounds."

Tufts of badger-grey hair stuck out from beneath his tweed cap. His tweed sports jacket needed a brush from dog hair and mud. The culprit for that was his dark brown and impractical longhair dachshund called Marmy, short for Marmite. Her pleading eyes were locked on my pork pie.

"Cock Low," said Anthony.

I wiped my dribbling nose on a paper napkin. "Pardon?"

"Cock Low, Cat Low, Grub Low. Bronze age burial mounds at Leek, Dilthorne, and Asbourne respectively. Cock Low's gone. Levelled by the county council for a mill. Now the mill's gone too and it's become damn all. A kids' playground."

"And?"

"Hear me out… Yes, Marmy. He does love you. And he *will* give you some of his pork pie. Stop dribbling… When Cock Low got destroyed the local vicar saw a double-lipped urn fall from the diggings. The urn smashed, of course, but in it were a very rare heart-shaped stone, an iron ring, and a parcel of chopped-up animal bones and parts of a child's skull. What you make of that, eh? Interesting?"

"Hm-hm. Ironic with the kids' playground. But for a mound to enthral it should be huge and have something square-walled on top," I said. "Castles are like that. I do like castles." It was that simple. Affection began early. Holidaying in Southern Ireland I played hide and seek with my parents among Doe Castle's empty ruins. Well, I hid until Dad shouted "For God's sake, boy. We'll be late for your mother's lie down!"

Then a stranger held my ankles so I could to kiss the Blarney Stone. Germs weren't a consideration. Formative happiness.

"Did you know Mary Queen of Scots played billiards in Tutbury Castle?"

Anthony snorted in disbelief. Typical lawyer. Never believe the truth, despite a mate telling it to their face.

Mary had been a captive at the castle large enough to be more like a fortified town than a fortress, occupying its wooded hill. A waxwork of her in a black dress sits there beside some candles under a red canopy bearing her royal coat of arms in the Julius Tower, a nineteenth-century folly which stands on the motte mound. Of her many prisons Tutbury was the one she most hated, being held captive here under Queen Elizabeth I on four occasions.

The castle straddles a site inhabited for over three thousand years. Iron Age defensive ditches encircle the main defensive hill. John of Gaunt, third son of King Edward III, and the chap describing England as "this precious stone in a silver sea", had the castle itself built in the fourteenth century. A Dutch surveyor reported in 1559 it was virtually falling down and indifferently repaired.

Mary dubbed Tutbury as sitting squarely on top of a mountain in the middle of a plain, entirely exposed to all the winds and "injures" of heaven. She wrote of winter horrors. The ancient structure, mere wood and plaster, admitted every draught – that "méchante vieille charpenterie", as she put it, through which the wind whistled into every corner of her chamber.

It was also extremely damp. Magnificent views of the Peak District included a large marsh right below. Where today iron-toothed cogwheels of old disused sluice gate workings rust, malevolent fumes arose. Foul enough for anyone, especially for a woman of Mary Stuart's delicate constitution. Which wasn't helped one iota by the body of a Catholic hung from a turret facing Mary's window, warning against her hearing Mass in secret.

It's the fodder for hauntings. And, in August 2015, news from Tutbury hit the *Daily Mirror*. Professional ghost hunters had caught a supposed phantom on film while recording the TV series 'The Past Hunters', a vehicle for psychic medium star Derek Acorah. Eerie footage shows a seeming apparition. Stood motionless against a wall for about twenty seconds, then silently it drifts across the room and out of sight. Cue much excitement and body clinging. The castle's website states:

> *"Wearing a full suit of armour, and behaving in a manner that might best be described as authoritative, this ghostly figure has been seen stepping out in John of Gaunt's Gateway and bellowing "Get thee hence!"*

On film not a word was uttered apart from: "Definitely a shadow there" … "It's moving" … and "OmiGod!"

Mary's ghost, if there is one, will have delighted in the castle, the last Royalist bastion in the county during the English Civil War, being slighted to fair nothingness by Cromwell's Parliamentarians in 1648.

Spirits aside, for me, Tutbury's fascination lies from well before Mary's incarcerations to a time beyond. I'm on about the Minstrel Court in the age of the "Minstrels' King". It is pigeonholed legal history dating back to good old John of Gaunt that prompts Anthony to lift an eyebrow of interest.

Despite the castle's ruination the court met there until the eighteenth century. The date was always on the mid-August Feast of the Assumption – the celebration of when the Blessed Virgin Mary's sinless soul and non-decomposed body was physically raised into Heaven. The jury's still out why the minstrels chose that particular day for their court. However the romantic notion of angelic harp and trumpet sounds must have appealed to the minstrels' sense of occasion.

Several 1381 transcriptions of John of Gaunt's Charter to the King of Minstrels exist. The court's functions were administrative and punitive. A jury called the 'Gentlemen of the Inquests' was appointed, drawn by lot. Being 'King' was also down to pot-luck, a contest between the previous year's stewards. Another of whose number was given the job to deliver a lengthy speech covering the origins of the court and the noble art and theory of music.

The jury then passed judgement, imposing fines or 'amercements' on any minstrels brought before the court for bad behaviour.

Naughties included:

> "Drunkenness profane cursing & swearing using lewd or obscene Songs playing to any company or Meetings on the Lords Day or by any other vice or immorality … [and] Whether any of them have intruded into any Company unsent for or played for any mean or disgraceful Rewards."

Once the punishments were dished out there was feasting followed by the day's highlight, the annual bull run.

An unlucky bull, the Prior's gift, was docked of its tail. And horns cut, its nose was blown full with cracked pepper. Then, pointed at Derbyshire on the far bank of the Dove, it was slapped hard on the rump. If any minstrel could catch the beast before it had splashed across the river they could claim it as theirs. Then what? Playing lute tunes on a Cannock street, cap on pavement, helped out by the imploring eyes of something hugely unusual?

Marmy, insulted by my meagre morsel of pastry began directing her dribble at Anthony's brogues. "Yes, yes, lovely. I know. He's a mean, mean man. We'll have to find you a nice sausage on our walkies."

Keep the dog in shape, I thought. Draining the last of my ale and grabbing a wodge of napkins I prepared for exercise.

Downhill, via the chip shop, and over a stile and we were on the shaggy sausage dog bliss of a cricket pitch. Anthony targeted the river – Staffordshire's until midway across. Oh my, oh my, the river. A pair of swans dipped heads in salute. Marmy yapped "Hello, to you, too," and sent coots scooting. A kingfisher flashed blue.

Where some twiggy branches touched the shaded water Anthony pinched off a nibble of warm banger and, much to Marmy's chagrin, plopped it in. "Watch," he said.

Splash. "How to cheer up a chub. They're sun-shy, you know."

I nodded affirmation. Just one of those random things you pick up. "For them this is a paradisiacal county." With encouragement chub grow up to 6 pounds.

Downstream lay a weir concocting low thunder and fast shallow runs.

Upstream, and a tributary of the Dove, cuts the Manifold.

A cornucopia of Stone Age odds and bobs in the Manifold caves just above the watermark had Anthony eulogising about ancient mineral miners. Unquestionably, if it's a cave you're looking for there is none more spectacular than Thor's. To see it, tip your head back to the sky Gods. The rock into which the cave burrows upraises like a giant grey fang. Dominating the valley it's an impressive landmark. Nature's a clever sculptor.

A puff to climb up to, the 33-foot wide cave mouth opens onto an echoing cathedral-high cavern, water hewn from Carboniferous limestone, recommends torch and rugged footwear.

Touching the imagination of Ken Russell, here he filmed dark, slippery scenes for his fang-profuse, phallic farce *The Lair of the White Worm*. Fantastical nonsense from 1988 maybe, yet, in Thor's Cave, bones of extinct animals are rooted out. Humans hunkering down began as long as ten thousand years ago and lasted until Saxon times. The broken bottles, litter, and a German seeking a 'handy' signal are more recent.

Beneath, in the river valley, spoil banks at Ecton date from when the lead and copper mines were some of the Country's richest.

The actual jewel of the Manifold Valley is at the southern end. Ilam. An eco-friendly place, it was first in Britain to abolish the old-fashioned light bulb. Here Manifold meets Dove. Evoking an England of the romantic soul are picture-postcard views across to Thorpe Cloud. And short crow's flight will alight upon Dovedale's popular stepping stones.

Ilam's orderly steep-roofed Swiss-chalet style homes give an Alpine aspect. I have to pinch myself agreeing with Arthur Mee, one time literary editor of the *Daily Mail*. The church font is a wonder, "so old that it is Saxon or Norman, the round bowl carved with humans and dragons". Only yards from the church is Ilam Hall in whose ground the Manifold River rises after going underground at a swallow-hole, a gurgle away from Wetton Mill tea-rooms.

The Manifold was distant in the direction two blokes, one carrying a dog, walked. Drowsy elderflower overhung water that was slow and deep. "Look, look trouty-trouts, Marmy!

"Sausage!" screamed the wriggling pooch, gulping only fresh air as reward from Anthony, happy as a larrikin.

More pale meat sank into the Dove. "Such super fish on this river stretch," Anthony gushed. "As if their faces morphed with freshwater prawn, whisker-faced Barbel have a real feel for sausage. It helps them put on the pounds, often as much as twenty. Name's from the Latin for beard."

"*Barba*, I know." I sounded snappish – the after-effect of the Dancing Duck perhaps.

"Only saying," said my friend cautiously, returning to topic. "Food-wise goofy grayling are the finickiest. No sausage for them. But what beauties! Their red standard's a whacking great floppy dorsal fin. Gnarly fishers say there's pike. I'll believe that should I ever see one." Marmy did a predatory impersonation. Her patience exhausted, she snatched what remained of the sausage from Anthony's fingers and with a leap fled behind my heels.

"Traitorous animal, I'll inter you with Mary Queen of Scots," Anthony laughed.

"Better that than a barrow mound?" I offered, climbing a stile, my napkin reserves disintegrated, to discover Marmy entangled in the only thorny obstacle before open countryside.

Stafford. Home of the Stafford Knot. Home, too, of Wild John.

He clicked his tongue. "Ethelfleda the eldest daughter of Alfred the Great had a stronghold here. She defended it against the Danes. The Stafford motto: "The Knot Unites" is down to her. Symbolically she stripped off her girdle and declared to a trio of local lords: "With this girdle, I bind us all as one". The lords' lands became Staffordshire."

"A girdle, really?"

"Really. And this big tump's worth it for nobbut the view," Wild John attested. His way of subtly broaching that the county town's castle isn't what it seems. Cute red squirrels once garrisoned it. So tame they could be hand fed suggests an essentially peaceable place.

Yes, the earthworks are Norman, sculpted from a glacial deposit – a sound base from whence Lord Robert de Tosny could tax the surly Saxons. The keep's single storey walls of stone and sections of brick that echo with cooing pigeons are not, however, the originals. They are nineteenth century Gothic revivalist – the reduced vision of Sir William Jeringham. I say reduced because in living memory the army took down three storeys for safety's sake.

At the minute the castle's the property of the local authority. And it's done some prettification. A large green and yellow sign thirty yards from the castle's visitor centre points to an ex-gravel pit. 'Medieval Herb Garden' is a smidge of a fib. The planting is fairly recent. 'Lurgy Beating Herbs' is a better evocation. Sage, for example, was a cure-all. Spearmint helped "stinking of the mouth". If depressed, sleep on a thyme-stuffed pillow. Garlic was recommended for cancer, leprosy, and colds. The mediaeval upper class shunned its use. The peasantry believed it the wonder bulb.

Back yonder the pukka keep had included five grand towers. Commanded built by Ralph, first Earl of Stafford, in 1347, the whole got demolished by Parliamentarians right before Christmas 1643 – an unseasonal slap on the wrist for a plucky defender.

Royalist Lady Isabel Stafford had done her best. But six weeks on the back foot became somewhat wearying. Thankfully, she did have "good and abundant" water. The keep had a well one hundred and sixty feet deep. Discovered accidentally in 1819 it was covered in oak and planks and under three feet of rubbish.

What her soldiers guarded had grown to bumper nettle, bramble, and hazel – and hello squirrels.

Yet Isabel's heroism was a bout of second billing amid the general ignominious nip and tuck of the English Civil War. Like counties elsewhere, Staffordshire contrived to tear itself apart willy-nilly, and carried on stubbornly doing so years after defeated King Charles hid in a Boscobel Wood oak tree on the border with Shropshire, prompting the War's official end.

But for now let's stick to 1643. Bombastic happenings at Lichfield, next at Hopton Heath, and then at Lichfield again, wreaked carnage worthy of special mention. Parliament, anxious to break the Royalist hold on the Midlands, advanced on Lichfield because it commanded the main north-south road through Staffordshire. The town's only defendable place was the cathedral – the Close being encircled by a high wall and moat. Royalist cannon and ammunition got stuffed into the house of God itself.

Just as the first primroses quivered Parliament laid siege and soon had a setback. Their leader, the radical Puritan peer Lord Brooke, was shot through the eye and killed by 'Dumb Dyott', a young deaf and dumb sniper and son of local gentry. It was a cracking aim from the cathedral's central spire. Divine judgment, said the Royalists. On the celebration day of Lichfield's patron saint St Chad, Brooke had denounced cathedrals as haunts of the Antichrist. Despite the trophy slaying within two days the Royalists surrendered. This alarmed King Charles and he ordered Lichfield be recovered pronto.

Parliament meanwhile set its sights on Stafford. A fortnight after Dumb Dyott's plumb musket ball the armies clashed just 3 miles to Stafford's north-west, at Hopton Heath. A place of rough ground great for a rabbit, not so good if a cavalry horse. And there were one thousand two hundred of those. Hedges and field walls provided Parliament musketeers with natural breastworks. The Royalists were forced to play their ace, 'Roaring Meg' – a heavy demi-cannon. It did the job and gave the massed cavalry a gift of an opportunity. After two charges the Parliament horse had skedaddled, its artillery was overrun, its infantry was almost routed, and many a gun was captured.

Unfortunately for the Royalists they too went and lost their leader. Unhorsed during the second charge, the Earl of Northampton became bloody-minded. He refused to surrender to "base rogues". A skull-splitting halberd blow put paid to his arrogance. Satisfied, the Parliamentarians made an orderly dusk retreat taking the Earl's corpse with them to parade through the streets of Derby.

Which still left the small matter of Lichfield. What occurred might explain why the city became one of few places to later get allocated a large government grant for CCTV cameras.

Replacing the slain Earl was Prince Rupert. The cathedral turned into a veritable fortress, he decided not to ponce about. He called up fifty loyal Cannock Chase miners. Draining the moat they made tunnels crammed with gunpowder up to the Close walls. On 20 April, BOOM! The first explosive mine to be used in an English siege had been detonated. The breech was massive – "wide enough for six men to enter abreast." The Parliamentarians surrendered quick-as-a-flash.

Pride hurt, Cromwell wanted the cathedral back. He got his wish. Pity the heavy gun barrage collapsed the central spire. Put it down to the ebb and flow of small defeats and victories that Lady Isabel found herself embroiled in.

"Unique." "The magnificent twin spires." The cathedral's tourist bumf is effusive nowadays. But oh, how much it could have been bettered but for naughty Cromwell's vandalism.

Celia Fiennes rode into Stafford in 1698 and wrote in her diary:

> "… an old built town, timber and plaister pretty much, in Long peaked Rooffes of tileing; 3 gates to the town-there was another wch Leads to the Castle wch now is ruinated, and only remaines on a hill the fortification trenches yt are grown over wth green. Ye streetes are pretty Large and well pitched; a broad space for ye market place Wherein is a good Market house on stone pillars wth a handsome town hall over it-some of the houses are pretty good. This Country is much for Entertainments, in every house you must Eate and drinke."

Hardly half awake, I hadn't even had a coffee when I chucked a quid of sympathy into a near empty acoustic guitar case of the day's human-interest story. Teenage and talented the bouffant-barnet busker sang 'Hallelujah, I Love You So' to a Stafford Community TV video camera outside Boots. An ogling fan club of five motley girls gobbled Greggs' pies and sausage rolls. He could barely afford the latter for breakfast going by mine and the other donations.

I pondered if he had considered a sex change. A female busker, it's claimed, earns three times more on average what a bloke does in the same place, playing the same songs, at the same time of day.

Maybe the advertising would help. Cobbled together from felt tips, Pritt stick, and scissors a large poster appealed finding him on YouTube, Soundcloud, Facebook, Twitter, and gawd knows what other social platforms.

Still, my morning's first sweet-talking enquiry "Can I *please* see Staffordshire's favourite son?" brought me face to face with Doctor Samuel Johnson. His portrait hangs in the grand 'Judge's Room' in Stafford's County Buildings. Looking a tad demented scowling in a black gown, his hands appear tense as claws. A book pile and a scroll prominent behind him, hint at a literary chap. He was much more, despite his annotated edition of *The Plays of William Shakespeare* suggesting a definite Bard of Avon fan if ever there was one. His quips were worth listening to – especially: "I am willing to love all mankind, except an American."

This was the man whose wet-nurse gave scrofula, a disease with glandular swellings, probably TB of some sort. Once it was called 'King's Evil' because only the royal touch might cure it. Queen Anne tried and failed. Hence the name, I suppose.

The tall toughie blind in one eye and deaf in one ear also suffered from Obsessive Compulsive Disorder and from Tourette's Syndrome. His odd gestures and tics caused William Hogarth to think him an idiot on first meeting.

A committed Tory he was given a stamp of approval by prolific scholar Pat Rodger as "arguably the most distinguished man of letters in English history". Rodgers failed to mention Johnson was also one of the country's last professional jesters. And likely the only one buried in a wood.

Born in 1691, his place of birth isn't known. A dancing master to local middle class families in his younger years, he rapidly gained a reputation as a wit, a poet, musician, and playwright. His play *The Supernatural* earned rave London reviews in 1729, Johnson himself playing the character Lord of the Flame.

Fame went to his head, itching that locals refer to him as "Lord". They did as bade, but behind his back called him "Maggotty", an old term meaning having maggots in the brain. Basically, being a crank.

Tummy rumbling, I almost, almost hoped Maggotty's contemporary competition in eccentricity would feed me Staffordshire specialities as vowed.

For all that, it wasn't purely the reason I followed my bonnet to Wild John's where, hospitable to a fault, he proved good as his word: pobs followed by fried frogs. The latter was fried sliced spuds. The former was toast and milk. That the full fat milk bordered on sour wasn't part of the recipe. "Yum, burnt bread and kefir," I said.

John had his excuses. "While you've been swanning around and putting your feet up with a laptop in the Australian sun your uni friends have been going through mid-life crises. Loneliness is worse when you return to it after a reprieve." Focused on a heaped frying pan of sizzling frogs he accentuated his sorrow with a cheek-chew. "See if you can find the ketchup."

After another quite long 'fling' John and Liz were again no longer an item. She was now somewhere on Staffordshire moorland enjoying teapot rituals, and, according to John, "Behaving like a prima donna over McDonalds".

He put the blame squarely on Kate Bush's escapist 'Wuthering Heights'. Liz had loved the song. Today, on John's kitchen floor, the visibly scratched vinyl record had the cat's food bowl sitting on it.

The only music to entertain warbled from a digital radio disguised in a retro wood-effect case which was tuned to the local community radio station, Windmill Radio.

Funnily enough it does broadcast from a windmill. Protuberant at Broad Eye, it wasn't far, a short stroll along the Sow riverbank. Along the length, coot upon coot dive under lily pads. Ducks and swans drift. Mirror carp make ripple rings. And alder and drooping willow thrive.

Since having the sails removed in 1897 the stone-built mill had several metamorphoses. It served as a butchers' shop before it was boarded up, derelict, having sycamore and ash growing on the inside along with miscellaneous wildlife. The radio station idea germinated in the '90s after *Blackadder's* Baldrick aka Tony Robinson, finding his feet with Channel 4's *Time Team*, and with the help of volunteers saved the mill from demolition.

"You'll find your homework is on the table," Wild John said. "Don't put sticky fingers on them. They're precious minor masterpieces. Signed first editions." Gingerly I went to pick up two tomes. *The First Book of Jabez* and *The Second Book of Jabez*.

"On second thoughts, don't touch. You can look at them when we get back."

The semi vertical walk to the top of Stafford Castle's motte, allowing for distracting summer doses of Shakespeare, expanded the lungs and made him feel top of the world. So Wild John said. Would do me good too, he cajoled.

"Lead on," I said – an autumn day politeness bereft of performance. Any indigestion, whether from brunch or lunch, I had to cope with.

Thus from the foot of the faux keep atop the grassy height the oppressive pewter sky was big and the landscape vast. I leaned on my Brasher hiking stick letting the lactic acid settle in my legs. Making a Moleskine note to the effect "The Bard's plays acted on open air stage below ancient walls above the clouds", had to wait a moment or two.

They were martyrs for the arts those players, deserving applause simply for putting up with frequent soakings never mind the soliloquies. Audience favourite *Much Ado About Nothing* seemed inappropriate. However, Wild John and I had climbed much higher than the empty stage below us.

Behind me was the M6. In front, over the tops of beech trees, I couldn't fail to identify the tower block. Pennycroft Court flats. Dominating the town centre like a middle finger raised at local tourism, it's Stafford's tallest building. Within this depressing den of drug-taking, spilt booze, smashed doors and windows, graffiti, and where homeless men sleep in store cupboards, a depressed woman hanged herself with her scarf from the stairwell, scrambling journos and other harbingers of doom.

Beyond the flats: the County Hospital – a further twelve hundred unnecessary deaths. The jaw quivers at the patients that lay in pain and filth, and crying for water. "A gross and terrible breach of trust," said Sir Hugh Keogh, medical director of the NHS.

The far horizon was the easier on the eye – the pastoral edge of Cannock Chase, 26 square miles of scenic heathland and deciduous and plantation woods. Turf where paranormal investigators occupy themselves with prowling monsters they believe follow tracks of fallow and red deer. Well, certainly something seems to cause the deer to get thumped by cars.

On balance, I was happy where I was for now.

"You won't get me up in one those. Not for all the Pedigree beer in the brewery," commented Wild John, gesturing toward a soaring glider.

A glass and carbon fibre affair, it had to be from the gliding club at Seighford, not far to the north-west. Once a wartime RAF base, its pre-fab huts transmogrified into family units for "displaced persons", a euphemism for Polish refugees. A camp of huts was also provided at Little Onn, not far from Leek, where Dyta, my wasp-waisted and lovely university dalliance, was baptised in the chapel. Deconsecrated, that now stores silage for cattle.

Oh yes, high on the national political agenda the Poles had flooded in. Immediately after 1945 approximately one hundred and thirty-five thousand went straight onto farms and building sites, or into the mines.

The reasons were twofold. Winston Churchill's declared in the House of Commons:

> "Her Majesty's government will never forget the debt they owe to the Polish troops who have served them so valiantly and for all those who have fought under our command."

And the Polish Resettlement Act provided entitlement to employment as well as unemployment assistance.

The Poles brought their culture. Traditional dress – floral headbands and colourful folk skirts, gorsetka and sukmana, and badger-skin sacks – was ever the stuff of festivals such as Corpus Christi and the 3rd of May – the calendar date celebrating Poland having the first democratic constitution in Europe. And as things are now, Stafford's White Eagle Polish Club stays focused on the strong sense of established community.

As for the gliding club, formed in 1963, it used the part of Seighford airfield that wasn't put down to Polish-planted vegetables.

Among the first club members was Walter Harvey, a raw beginner. Within three years he could glide the thermals like a buzzard, five hours at a time. A chap with a bladder of steel, I imagined.

But at least a glider was a glider and not some UFO.

In 1964 a UFO was seen crashing in a field. The field was cordoned off. Officials from Air Force intelligence and NATO investigated. Incident reports say, "three bodies were recovered" and taken to Wiltshire's infamous Porton Down Scientific Research Centre. Local eyewitness Harold South told reporters he saw "a Delta shape item covered in tarpaulin and lifted onto an Aircraft Transporter". Harold had his camera confiscated by police forthwith.

And I recalled excited Stafford residents inundating the local BBC station on Saturday, 27 July 2008 to report new sightings. Up to eighteen lights were in the night heavens, some moved then stood stock-still. Some appeared to be in formation, some random. My giddy aunt! The official explanation of Chinese lantern style balloons released after a party didn't curry local favour.

A Ministry of Defence report cited Stafford as a UFO activity 'hotspot'.

And in hindsight de-classified Government documents dated from 1986 to 1992 give accounts of silent balls of light circling the Pye Green tower – built during the Cold War as a backup communication system on fear of a Soviet electromagnetic pulse attack. A 10-foot light hovered over the Stafford Road. And cigar-shaped tubes flew over Burntwood. Letters sent between MoD officers and Staffordshire Police attempted explanations. Chinese lanterns? Pull the other one.

Wild John stamped his feet. Potters, even those in spirit, were down to earth people. No matter how wealthy or successful, they chose to spend life in a hovel. Well, that was Wild John's little joke, a hovel being the character-ful bottle-shaped brick building enclosing a kiln. He knew all the old potters' terms. One-legged dancer and jollyer, pugman and cod placer were but a few.

More useful though, was him being an expert on Staffordshire dialect.

Any hunch that 'duck', 'shug', and 'up Hanley' had been enough lingo for me to muddle through was to hoodwink myself. A proper adult education would be nice. Hence, I'd earmarked Wild John for tutelage.

I hasten to add he had mellowed – there was less of the 'wild'. Although still self-guiding his crew cut in the blood-speckled bathroom mirror, he finger-plucked his guitar rather than thrashed it. And his penchant for wasting away dark inactive days being artistically miserable over Liz kicking him into touch again was passé. No longer did he shout at shadows or cuddle the poetry of Bertolt Brecht while listening to the David Bowie 'Baal' EP on the turntable.

He had though kept his ska records and become one of those fine fellows who take it upon themselves to keep important things alive for reasons of having nothing else better to do.

A rummager by nature, his vocabulary of Staffordshire dialect words borders on the expansive. For instance he eats his 'salary', as opposed to celery.

The catalyst had been a scrapbook filled over the years with *May Un Mar Lady* cartoon strip treasures that first appeared on 8 June 1985. A drawn microcosm of Potteries' domesticity, the strip featured a middle-aged married couple captioned in 'Pots' dialect – a daily smile in a little black and white box on the inside pages of the *North Staffordshire Evening Sentinel* for eighteen seamless years.

John revelled in it. Recalling, it sometimes took him twenty minutes to decipher the gist and puzzle out a punchline. An undemanding example of the banter presents the kind of bother:

(Her) "Thay anna got a crowbar in th' shed ast?"

(Him) "Neow, I anna …. Ennyreowd whut dust want a crowbar fer?"

(Her) "Ter lever thay iter thut damn cheer thayst bin stuck in o' dee!"

In a nutshell, the wifey asks her hubby if there's a crowbar in the shed to prise him out of the chair he's been sat in all day.

And to raise the bar:

(Him) "Eet neow good ah conna get to slay."

(Her) "At thay werritin abite th' rent bayin' thray wiks overdue, th' final demand fer the' reetes un 'ow way're gooin ter peey next months car instalment?"

(Him) "Nar... ther's a rumour thut th" Potters Arms is ggin ter cleowse dine!"

To paraphrase: the hubby can't get to sleep. The wifey asks if he's worrying about the rent, the final rates demand, or the HP on the car. No, he wasn't. Instead, it was the worrying rumour the local pub was closing down.

It's witty, gentle stuff that conned a generation. The enigma of the Pots lingo was one the artist Dave Fellows found incapable of writing himself. A translator had been a necessity. The biggest swizz was Dave loosely basing *May Un Mar Lady* on his own parents. And where did the Fellows family hail from? Stafford.

The problems began after five years when the translator retired. Dave thought, "Well that's the strip gone".

"Can't you do the dialect?" asked a newly appointed editor.

"Nooo! You're joking!" said Dave.

"Have a go, anyway," the editor encouraged. Dave did. Going through all the back strips he found all the keywords, made himself a phrase book, and took it from there until he passed on in October 2003.

But there were letters. Nasty ones. It has to be remembered some people still use a strong Potteries accent even now. Seldom do the younger generation realise that the accent even varied from town to town. Difference existed between say Burslem and 'Neck End' – which is Longton to the non-native like me – home to another of Dave's imaginings captioned by Alan Povey, *Owd Grandad Piggot*.

Longton was also the home, I must add, of Russell Crowe's fancy that, in 1953, emerged from a Gladstone Works kiln, today the last untouched example of a North Staffordshire potbank. The Kiwi star of *The Water Diviner* – a known collector of Staffordshire teacups – took to Twitter trying to get hold of a rare Queen Elizabeth Coronation souvenir mug. Among the million plus followers to read his tweet was Nerys Williams, a Gladstone Pottery Museum worker. Back she tweeted with a photograph of just the thing at the museum.

The suggestion is that due to the North Staffs area's past isolation the local accent is very close to Old English with its Anglo-Saxon base. Anthony Bunn, once editor of Stoke fanzine *A View To A Kiln* asked: "Are we in the midlands or the north?" Geographically, the midlands, he reflected, but probably the Stokie identifies more with the northerner. The accent is pretty unique. The more unenlightened and uneducated confuse it as a mix of Yorkshire, Scouse, Brummie and Mancunian. When used in its broadest sense, hip southerners can't understand a blinking word.

But give a native dialect speaker *Sir Gawain and the Green Knight* to read, it suddenly changes from incomprehensible to a lilting poem as it was constructed to be. This has led scholars to speculate that a creative monk from Dieulacres Abbey, near Leek, quill-penned it.

The Potteries accent is much more difficult to imitate than say Geordie or West Country. Few actors from outside the Potteries have managed to master it. The 1976 TV series *Clayhanger* is a good example. Not one actor involved gave a passable rendition.

Dave, however, admitted his solo efforts at dialect began badly. "It was so awful. There's a certain rhythm to it. I didn't get it right at all. Although Stafford dialect's pretty broad."

Wild John would be the first to agree. He's gleeful that Dave's *May Un Mar Lady* has waxed into a new local radio show *Oi, Get Yer Own Oatcake*!

Asked what on earth possessed him to start up a strip, Dave had laughed: "Don't know!" In fact it stemmed from he and his brother coming to Stoke-on-Trent for a drink on a Friday. "We'd never ever go in a pub and end up on our own," he expounded. "Somebody would always come and sit by you and talk to you, which is unheard of in Stafford. I mean, you could be dead in a pub in Stafford and nobody would take any notice."

That truth quite tickled Wild John, who squidged a teabag in a mug each of milky piping-hot water to hit the spot after our downhill return. The mugs were worth a read. Moorland's Pottery had seen potential in the loyal Stokie – even an honorary one. "Ay Up Ow At Oraight," said my mug. "Cost kick a bo agen a wo an yed it till it bosts," said Wild John's. Why should I have been surprised when his mobile rang with a Stokie dialect ringtone. The voice of Howard Reynold.

Wild John lunged for the phone and looked disappointed. "I've got windows already, and on my PC, " he said. The call abruptly ended, he muttered: "Always hopeful it might be Liz."

"You should wipe the cobwebs off her Brown Betty," I said, gesturing to a teapot in dark kitchen niche.

"Will. One day."

Rehydrated and hands tissue wiped, I stretched awkwardly for a Jabez. Whole chunks about a fellow thinking himself as a countryman living in the industrial Potteries' shadows were maddeningly incomprehensible. The writer William Bloor took the pen name 'A Scott'. Must have been his way of rubbing along, him being a principal scientific officer of the British Ceramic Research Association.

Printers to whom he sent his first manuscript wanted to be paid the premium rate. It was customary to do this ... for articles written in a foreign language. Unsurprising with words such as 'chopsing' and 'cunny-fogle', 'fow staith' and 'grey nice'.

Jabez was one of those organic characters one feels lucky to come across in village life. And he had all the genuine "pott'ry' man's" contempt for snob-bery and artificiality. Of sturdy build, he had a face "best described as craggy, eyebrows which were distinctly bushy, and small but bright blue eyes that betrayed a roguish sense of humour".

His everyday clothes, Sunday excepted, "were a nondescript jacket and a pair of 'moleskin' trousers, the legs of which were tied just below the knee with string or pieces of old bootlace" – a common practice among miners at that time.

Like Wild John, Jabez had a preference for a collarless shirt. His trapping included a spotted nerkerchief, glasses on the end of his nose, and a curvy walking stick. "In spring and summer Jabez would be carrying a posy of wild flowers," imagined Bloor. "These were delightful arrangements, about six inches or so across, having the general shape of a large mushroom."

I slid the Jabez back on the table.

"You'll never guess Bloor's sons bunged those two books together and Keele published them as a Centenary Compendium."

"Absolutely never would," I said. It was time to take my leave. "Which is the quickest way to Stoke from here?"

"Until they build HS2? Follow the painted M6 sign Nouth."

"And that's dialect for ..."

"Isn't for anything. Someone from Severn Trent utilities couldn't spell. A company spokesman stated: "mistakes happen." And blamed "haste". True, probably. Our artisan couldn't wait to get the hell out of school."

"More like CNSQNS," I offered.

"Which is?"

"Central Nervous System Quantity Not Sufficient... Reckon it's going to happen, HS2?" The real possibility of High Speed Two, the ultra-rapid railway link from London to Birmingham, the East Midlands, and points north beyond, getting the green light was a worry.

Wild twiddled his thumbs for a moment or two. "Supposed to be cutting through swathes of our countryside without a stop. Think of it. Ancient mossy woodland split and splintered. Vicar's Coppice, Ravenshaw Wood, Black Slough, Tomhay Wood, and Big Lyntus." He counted the names off on his fingers. "Poor bloody squirrels. Then Madeley and Whitmore Heath. Whoosh! 'Maximise the opportunities for the greater economic sub-region,' that's the corporate bullshit. But no, it won't happen."

He had my rapt attention. "Why not?"

"London's Primrose Hill. To get to Euston the concerned community's hearts and minds must be won over. That'll be effing impossible. At the last moment the whole thing'll be scrapped."

I wished I shared his confidence.

Meantime, Stoke – that "swamp for the dying trees of the pottery industry" – was 18 miles away. Nouth.

Bobble Hat and Strumpet

"Every bird as it is reared and the lark for the bog."
Irish Proverb.

"G'day, g'day, what's new cobber?" I asked in mock Aussie.

"Singledom," sighed Anna, softly as the August breeze.

I stopped playacting. "Whoah. How long?"

"A whole week. My fault. Couldn't cope a minute longer. Every year for the past twenty Stewy's been deserting me for dirty weekends in Wales. Just around our anniversary he buggers off without fail, apart from nineteen ninety-five when he moaned it was too dry. This year was really bad. He did it wearing a summer dress and an imitation Jimmy Choo handbag on his arm."

I tried to be delicate. "Has Stewy turned …?"

"No-no, not that ..."

"What then?"

Stood arms crossed, Anna gave a resigned sigh. "Bog snorkelling."

Happily this wasn't some loo perversion. Rather that Stewy immersed himself in a natural phenomenon – peat bog. Abounding with spiky rushes, moss carpets and stinky sog, Staffs has a lot of them, and all bog bush-cricket friendly – the grasshopper rather than a summer game variant.

Absorbingly, twenty per cent of the world's bogs are British and under more threat than tropical rainforests. A peat bog takes thousands of years to form. Trapping carbon aids against the 'grey nice' effect. Best Stewy was steered toward conservation. Him blowing steady spurts of liquefied bog from out his snorkel was surely akin to dredging.

Stewy's ears, however, were clogged. His annual 'addiction' – the Bog Snorkelling World Championship in Llanwrtyd Wells – was irresponsibly hailed by the Lonely Planet as one of the top fifty global "must dos". As a matter of course Stewy abided by the two simple rules: that entrants cannot use mainstream swimming strokes and forward propulsion is solely by flippers. Stewy had the additional encumbrance of fancy dress. And for this he deserved merit. It's no easy feat to jounce along a 133 metre trench. Especially in the zero visibility of a decomposed plant suspension described as, "crap tasting chocolate milk". Participants from across Europe, Australia, Japan, USA, and Canada end up only identifiable as swamp monsters. Spectators are legion and Ben and Jerry's the latest underwhelming sponsor.

"Stewy got beat by a pantomime unicorn," said Anna. "He blamed the handbag and got mopey. I yelled at him he'd lost sight of things more important and should go and jump in Chartley Moss and stay there."

"Ouch." Now that *was* somewhere off limits. Within yelling distance of Stowe-by-Chartley and its castle – a motte and bailey affair boasting a rare cylindrical keep – Chartley Moss is Britain's largest example of a floating peat bog. And it's blooming dangerous. Covering a hundred acres, the top surface of nine-foot thick peat floats on fifty-foot of water. Long submerged, ghostly legend claims, are a huntsman and his beagle pack – which might explain any damp nip in the air.

"Did your beloved do as told?" I asked, concerned.

"No, he's on Ruski Rodge's kine slice sofa in Bentilee."

"Oh … my … God. Er, what's a kine slice sofa?"

"Council house, you donk. And don't believe the propaganda. They're both perfectly safe."

"Yeah, sure. Behind locked and bolted doors."

Bentilee. A perceived den of urban iniquity and, strikingly juxtaposed, home of the kamikazi pheasant. I recalled 2012's coroner's verdict of accidental death suffered by a motor cycling music tutor – 1999's winner with his band Marlo of the BBC talent show *Get Your Act Together*. His helmet visor had the bird embedded in the manner of a dog's cone of shame.

The unhappy tale highlights that rural nature is close. The housing estate, lauded as Europe's largest when built in the 1950s, covers the land of two once perfectly viable dairy farms somewhere between Hanley and Longton.

Back in those days of smoke-smutted pigeon racing and bingo, a legion of small caterpillar-track bulldozers went to work. Their job was slum clearance. And suddenly the Potteries led the country in destruction. The hugger-mugger alleys, dark backs, and reported tales of open sewers, communal water taps and latrines could no longer be tolerated.

Dab hands at calculation submit that in the Potteries' salad days there were up to four thousand bottle kilns with smoky, coal fired ovens. Two thousand still stood in the 1950s. The Clean Air Act all but put paid to them. Gas and electricity was the accepted way forward.

Nobody could seriously regret the passing of the old squalor and ugliness that mushroomed from the unplanned industry that grew up in Victorian times. But there was nostalgia among Potteries' folk for the cosiness of the old terraces almost a step from bed to workbench.

By comparison the Bentilee estate seemed clinical and sterile to some. One working potter told a TV documentary crew hoovering vox pop opinion: "I don't want to move. I could live in any of the suburbs, my salary's such that I could afford it. But I don't want it. I want the folk that I live with. North Staffordshire folk. Stoke on Trent people that are nice to know."

He wasn't the only negative. "There not nowhere you can go," said a disenchanted girl of the dance-clubbing sort. The sort to have frequented Tunstall's 'Golden Torch', which should not be confused with Wolfgang Buttress' 'Golden', now the tallest sculpture in the country. That thrusts, pointedly as a vanilla pod and LED lit, into the North Staffordshire sky, and features one and a half thousand hand blown glass prisms, each containing a memory or wish written by local denizens on handmade paper.

The 'Golden Torch' was a raucous nightclub in a 'quiet' terraced street and credited with birthing the modern all-nighter. The queue for T-Rex and Black Sabbath, or to hear the latest rare 7-inch gem from the States, would straggle over 200 yards back to a sustaining chip shop.

Bentilee was, however, the most blatant of noble projects. A giant council estate plonked middle for diddle in the countryside had views of heathered hills, open fields and streams. Goodness, each red brick semi-detached had an upstairs en-suite bathroom and a downstairs loo, albeit tiny. Private ablutions were sorted. Naturally there were takers.

And clubs or no, outside the young and innocent, and not so innocent, had a paradisiacal playground.

As a whole, the estate was almost genius. Tasked over two years, cement mixers, bricklayers, roofers, joiners, glaziers, plumbers and sparkies did their stuff. Laid-out south to west, the sun was invited to bathe its light simultaneously into the front and back gardens. The latter let wet clobber dry and allowed for whiling away the odd hour watching cabbages grow. Inside, natural daylight spilled through a window at each end of the living room.

People wanted to live in the 'Sunshine Houses'. So much vitamin D would cure the rickets, without a shadow of a doubt.

Seven thousand arrived keen to fill two thousand five hundred and eighty-six homes. And all about them turned to claggy splodge when the clouds opened.

With mud and clay ankle-deep the building site had to be endured. Each day folk had two changes of shoes. Maybe more, if unlucky. Almost worthy of a bog-snorkel itself, the squelchy embankment of the estate-splitting brook caused the loss of many soles. Certainly, any trip to Hanley needed a spare pair of footwear in the planning.

Pushing prams was a proper hassle. The milkman, though, got the short-est straw. It would be five o'clock in the afternoon before he made his last delivery. But he wasn't the only caller, by far. Scores of door-to-door sales-men peddled everything from dishcloths to carpets, the bigger dunnage getting paid for by instalment. Or not. Defaulters hiding from the collectors earned Bentilee the name 'Dodge City'.

But a late 'pinta' or a boot in the door wasn't a real deterrent. Thousands more came, ballooning the new community to over four and half thousand properties in nice-sounding streets like Winchester Avenue and Devonshire Square.

And sprawled as it was across a thick coal seam dabbled with during the Industrial Revolution, heating the estate was a no-brainer. A back-to-back coal fire fed a built-in boiler. Sufficient heat then for the kitchen range, and verso the living room hearth. However, there was problem – a planner's botch. Metal window frames. Damp began to rise and, perhaps unrelated to the windows, so did crime.

Rarely does a day go by without adverse stories of Bentilee folk. I found five with a few glances through a stashed pile of the local newspaper.

For starters, a sketchy teen had parked his wheels in the sitting room of an end terrace house having driven through the wall. Then, an aging chick appearing at court wearing pink-rimmed specs and an outsize grey cardy couldn't defend the 7p barcode pulled from her bra used to buy pricey goods at Asda self-service tills.

And it got better.

A perfidious woman in her forties had been found guilty of benefit fraud after failing to tell the DWP about a £95,000 windfall won on the TV show *Deal or No Deal*.

A jailed bad egg described himself to an arresting police officer as 'the hardest man in Bentilee'. Having thumped his ex twice in the face, stamped on her head, and then kicked her in retaliation for supposedly biting his finger many might disagree with the scrote's self-portrait. Certainly, a Chinese gentleman did, opining in the readers' comments: "Castrate him and throw him down an abandoned mine shaft."

The fifth story badly soiled the reputation of a Staffordshire bull terrier. I mean, come on, image is important for a woofer with short, broad, almost triangular head that's vice-jawed and toothed. A woofer whose distant blood-line was encouraged into baiting rings to tenderise the meat of bulls.

But that was before an Old English Bulldog was crossed with a wimp. The latter was the English White Terrier, a pooch Rawdon Briggs Lee surmised in his 1894 book *Modern Dogs*, that "had been a fox terrier crossed with a white Italian greyhound". The description is striking: "most fragile and delicate", "not a sportsman's companion", "makes a nice house dog", "requires a considerable amount of cuddling and care." Natural selection made the mutt extinct. But some genes survived.

Voila, the loveable rogue of the dog world! Almost any Staffie will wag its hard tail and mug its owner with friendly purpose, strength and agility – assets fostered by Staffordshire's miners and ironworkers developing the breed's qualities of gameness, intelligence and loyalty in a fair exchange. Dogs were a source of pride and status.

According to a RSPCA vet writing in a 2011 edition of *K9 magazine*, "problems only occur when bad owners exploit the Staffie's desire to please by training them to show aggression".

And this explains how, in Bentilee, a Staffie was a noisy accomplice in the stabbing to death of 'Bugsy', an innocent Asian happening to be in the wrong place at the wrong time. Drunk, the perpetrator's excuse was being enraged because his taxi hadn't turned up.

Fact is it's simple to guess why the estate's now the most deprived district in Stoke-on-Trent. Ironic given the original intention. Never mind the graffiti. Bed-sheet sized flags of Saint George left hanging from upstairs windows provide patriotic decorations for those with no intention of being politically correct.

Juxtaposed is a Bentilee boxing club, in line for Sport England's 'Satellite Club of the Year' award for helping to reduce anti-social behaviour and cut racial tensions by bringing together diverse groups. Kids as young as four take part in sessions to make new friends and stay off the streets. And an eight-year old lad told a good news hunting journalist, "We've learned all the different punches, like upper cuts and hooks and I know how to stand the right way ... I came to train up and to help me protect myself if anyone picks on me at school."

"You remember Rodge?" said Anna, giving me a prod.

"Course I do. Russian Studies, Politics, and exotic tobacco. First came by train to Stoke on a late autumn afternoon and thought he'd arrived at Hell on Earth."

Safe to say Rodge's perception was on a par with past travellers' comments. Like the unattributed posh speaker in the 1964 ATV documentary *Gone But Not Forgot*: "My first impression of the Potteries was the view one gets travelling on the train from Derby to Crewe which was of the most revolting industrial wilderness I had ever passed through in my life."

Rodge wasn't posh. He just spoke his mind. "Government tends to be ivy that thinks it's the tree," was his favourite on-liner. I recalled his bohemian's mop of scruffy black hair, scraggy beard, black bobble hat, two sizes too big black greatcoat, and the Doc Martens; that his exhaled spliff smoke stupefied rooms; and he had 'a thing' for Dostoyevsky. Looking back on it, Anna had a crush on him. "So how is he?"

"Oh, you know. Divorce. Customs and Excise didn't work out. Socialist values. Affordable rent ... Grows beetroots, cabbages and stuff ... and sunflowers. Says he thinks of his home as 'Little Rostov' 'cos the Rostov region's home to a fifth of Russia's sunflower growing."

"Rodge tell you that?"

"Hm-hm. A while ago. Did you know Russian soldiers were sent off into the field with a two-pound sack of sunflower seeds as food? Rodge is collecting his seeds for a rainy day."

"Really? Any one in particular? Never thought of Rodge as a Bentilee horticulturalist. Then again ..."

"He has got one of the bigger gardens."

"A few elbows or worse used there, then, in the free for all land grab." Bentilee's first house occupiers finding unmarked plots as gardens of bare earth erected fences as they wished, or were persuaded. Housewives starting from scratch had literal meaning.

"Rodge makes the best of it. Always bubbles borsch on the stove ... but I really miss Stewy."

"So shall we go and say 'hello'?" Although having an odd compulsion to see the sunflowers, I almost hoped Anna would refuse my charitable suggestion.

After a pregnant pause she nodded. I steeled myself. "Glad I decided to dress down... Okay. Let's run the gauntlet."

"I'll be brave if you're brave. But it's cool. Bentilee's gone up-market. It's got a complex."

"So it bloody should."

"No, I mean *a complex*. *The Sentinel* says it's unique in the Country. There're shops, all kinds of brands, an IT centre, a walk-in health centre, a CAB, and ..." Anna giggled, "... probably just for Rodge, there's a library for his Pushkin, too."

So, with Anna sitting on Stewy's knee and a dozen sunflowers bowing heavy yellow heads out the open back door, I asked Rodge about Bentilee's villainous infamy.

"It's been totally overplayed and exaggerated," he said. "The stigma's not deserved. But at least my little amount of money bought a load of house and garden. It's a chuffing large place with a dense community, so obviously it reveals a higher proportion of crime. Reckon there's no more crime here than anywhere else – it's just that it's ... concentrated. C'mon, lets leave these two smoochers and go for a wander. I'll show you the new stone carvings. Sort of personal interest. They're not *too* far."

"So ... shall we go in the Fiat?"

"Errr."

A no, then. The vision was a nightmare – Milami jiggered to having bricks for alloys. A wander it definitely was.

"I'll lead the way," said Rodge, keenly. It's an easy stroll. Just up the Dividy Road ... That's the old Dividy Lane. Here long before the estate. Imagine hay wagons, pitchforks, and bodice-laced wenches ..."

"The fab proletariat," I said, making Stewy jerk with silent laughter, his tongue at bog snorkelling depth around Anna's tonsils.

Rodge nodded, over-enthusiastically adding: "Then over the Tiverton Road, and bingo. The carvings are on the edge of the Berryhill Fields. It's a lovely open space, the lungs of the Potteries. Full of owls, rabbits, bats and fish. And there's a stone circle – twelve sandstone lumps. Plus a flatty in the middle. Don't be fooled. The circle's not ancient. Millenium. Hanley's got one two. Same sort of age. But that's only five stones big. Though one stone's over 7-foot."

I asked Rodge if he got out a lot.

Still, the 170 odd acres of Berryhill grassland are worthy of comment. Close to the construction of the stone circle the foundations of an ancient dovecote, a chance discovery, drew tentative archaeological spades, trowels, and wheelbarrows.

More implements were summoned. Net curtains twitched in nearby Trimble Close. Something big was buried. The City Council and Groundwork Stoke-on-Trent bunged in money to swell Millennium Project funding, and proper excavations got organised. Keele University's History Department sent diggers and delvers.

A moated manor house was unearthed. BBC Two cameras captured the moment with presenter Rory McGrath nattering a commentary about the house dating almost back to Magna Carta and being occupied for two centuries. For Rory this was a bit of side-work to his mainstay, good old *They Think It's All Over*.

Someone gave the house a name: Lawn Farm Manor. A hunting lodge of importance, it was claimed. And mention was made of its Middle Ages deer park. The Black Death, however, oversaw the drastic downsizing of the community whose lord, in 1349, galloped off to Hertfordshire in an attempt to escape the nasty flu-like symptoms, enlarged lymph nodes and tummy pain scuttled ashore by ... gerbils, it's now believed. By my whiskers! Ratus ratus was innocent.

This said, the excavation of Lawn Farm was nowt compared to what could have been well after deer made way for canaries. Coal mining replaced the pastoral life. Fast forward to the 1980s. The ailing leviathan, British Coal, hatched a plan: opencast mine Berryhill Fields in their entirety. A fine way to offset pit closures, it said. Boasting it had never lost an application to opencast.

Aware that hungry gnawing of the black stuff would pretty much have reached the City centre, a jumbo community campaign was organised like the clappers. Barry Stockley, an erstwhile councillor, remembers: "one desperate fight to raise funds to engage the best counsel we could afford."

It went to appeal and the Coal Board was beaten. "We submitted over five thousand letters of support for our case," Barry reminisced. "Five thousand letters each individually written and composed so they couldn't say we had just collected signatures. I think this impressed the commissioner who heard the appeal at Stoke Town Hall in 1993. I can see *The Sentinel's* headlines now – 'Berryhill is Thrown Out!'" *The Sentinel* had roared into the battle of the Fields. The late edition carried daily bulletins.

The campaign's intensity inspired the New Vic Theatre's scruff-pot director Peter Cheeseman, once described by Simon Hoggart as the "furry caterpillar" because of his habitual woolly sweaters. His work was nourished by the social history and struggles of Stoke's industrial community. Cheeseman adjusted his spectacles, rubbed his beard in thought, and penned a new play.

And keeping true to the theatre's Potteries roots, *The Dirty Hill* wowed the nation's critics. Research had meant dispatching out his actors to obtain original material, using only the words spoken or written by the people involved in the actual events. Challenging, indeed. Rodge, of course, quoted me the Russian journalist Isaac Babel: "No iron can stab the heart with such force as a full stop put just at the right place."

Cheeseman, however, was even-handed in his stirring. Him ruminating with Hem Heath miners in 1981 produced *Miner Dig The Coal*, another of his famous 'documentary plays' drawing attention to local causes that began with *Jolly Potters*. Indeed, the local railways got the Cheeseman treatment in *The Knotty*. And steel, too, was worth a campaign. *Fight For Shelton Bar!* was a typical response to the threatened closure of the local steel works.

One thing Cheeseman stuck to his guns on was that actors mingle with the audience in the local pub after the show. Countering the aloof, cod "glamour" of the profession sometimes went down like a lead balloon, but most entered into the Brechtian spirit of the enterprise.

Come 2009, Cheeseman, by now a CBE for his services to drama, a DLitt, having had an Honorary degree bestowed by Staffordshire University, and retired, received the Young Vic award – an annual prize recognising outstanding contribution to theatre-making in the UK and for a lifetime's encouragement and inspiration to a younger generation. Film director Mike Leigh who was in the Vic company in the '60s had words to say about his friend: " The spirit in which we worked, to be political and truthful, was down to him. He was a genius, a vagabond, a facilitator. What he achieved is colossal."

Cheeseman's career spanned thirty-six years and more than one hundred and forty productions. Having their talents nurtured by him were Alan Ayckbourn, Bob Hoskins, Ben Kingsley and Robert Powell. Indeed, when Peter died in 2010, actor Powell said: "There are some people who are absolutely, totally responsible for me sitting here now, and Peter's at the top of page one."

It's pertinent to add that Cheeseman founded the Victoria Theatre in a defunct Stoke cinema with three hundred and forty-seven seats, for less than five grand. Helping him was Stephen Joseph, a stage director and the pioneer of "theatre-in-the- round" – a form of theatrical presentation in which the audience is seated on at least three of its sides.

Cheeseman pointed out that, "ordinary people had accepted the circus and the boxing ring for thousands of years, and the intimacy of theatre-in-the-round involved the audience in a totally new, absorbing way that was more true to real life." That was in 1962.

The year of the Coal Board's Berryhill Fields defeat the Vic moved to Newcastle-under-Lyme. With six hundred and five seats, this was the New Vic. Masterminded by Cheeseman, it's Europe's first purpose-built theatre-in-the-round.

And theatre unto itself, Rodge and I hit the Dividy Road. Pushchair-shoving, teenage honey monster mums shouted across the street at one another. "Heya, Shannon! "Hiya, Brittnay!" Undernourished youths, their arms around each other's shoulders and sharing a bottle of something to make the legs wobble, meandered about naked but for man-thongs and chunky gold necklaces. They hailed us with, "Bro, got any G? Speed, bro!" I looked at Rodge. He shook his head alarmingly as if trying to dislodge Black Death fleas.

I took a deep breath and we both quickened our step. Police officers of Operation Nemesis had been targeting suspected drug dealers. And hurrah, a quantity of "cannabis vegetation and cultivation equipment" had been seized. But it just took a piffling edge off the general headache. Drug problems are at an all time high. The electronic squelch of the early '90s rave scene has to take the brunt of the blame. Indeed, I knew of several guys holding memories of the Tittensor Beech Caves.

Visible from a small lane, the caves in a hilly wood were formed through pillar and stall workings in the 1630s when the red sandstone was quarried to build New Trentham Hall. Today the caves are covered with liberal graffiti that a local farmer tries to hide with manure heaps. The true legacy of the cave raves, however, are the stories of suicides and numerous overdoses. The stuff of urban legend, I suppose.

"Want to know something?" asked Rodge.

"Go on."

"Druggies around here stockpile their methadone prescriptions so they can sell them to buy heroin. Boots on Devonshire Square tries to stop that by doling out methadone to drink there and then. Doesn't quite work. Addicts regularly don't actually swallow the stuff. They keep in their mouths, run outside, spit it into a jar and resell it. The dealers themselves are unstoppable. One flat just up and across the road from me even used the downstairs window to sell drugs. It was like how we used to buy oatcakes."

"Surely Bentilee's got a core of good and decent folk." I countered.

"Totally right" Rodge agreed. "If only we could all live in Mow Cop. That's higher than Peter Crouch's eyebrows, and idyllically free from crime, litter, dog mess, unemployment, et cetera, et cetera. Let it be our Winterfell."

"And only filled with loving, non-judgemental people?" I chuckled.

Rodge couldn't suppress a smile. "Yeah, abso-bloody-lutely."

And following his lead we were at the carvings in no time. For all money the stones they adorned resembled the prehistoric. Sculpted by Peter Price and called 'Stone Gateway' they were chiselled from Hollington sandstone, stuff that's on his Cheadle doorstep and used to fashion churches and stately homes for centuries. Passionate about mediaeval gargoyles and the Green Man, Peter gave up being a pot-bank manager after teaching himself stone-masonry. And he's become quite prolific. The carvings around the Alton Towers Hotel entrance are also his.

As for 'Stone Gateway', three large boulders stood behind a block, smaller and lower, with chiselled sides to suggest a wall. Fine. It was intended to commemorate the Bentilee area before farmers settled a tidy time ago. A lizard, a bird, several snails, and a hunting scene of a pair of wild boar being chased by two men on foot were okay. There were, however, details that caused me to think Peter wasn't an historian – a girl with a ponytail in T-shirt and shorts and the head of a bearded, curly-haired figure appearing to wear a bobble hat.

"Don't you think the dude looks like me?" grinned Rodge, nibbling on a sunflower seed pinched from a recycled stash tin.

I couldn't help but chuckle. "A striking ancestral resemblance, maybe. The sculptor's got your hat to a tee. You still smoking the exotic stuff?"

"Not since Tony Edwards retired around the millennium," Rodge replied carefully. Gentleman Tony! The Welshman of 'smoker's paradise'! A former pilot, his reeking Fountain Square tobacconist shop J.M. Edwards – his mum's name – was venerated and gubbins full. Everything puffable was stocked – pipes, cigars, fags, and the flavoured tobaccos that Rodge was so partial to.

Adaptable, Tony was the founder member of the Association of Independent Tobacco Specialists. Curiously, he also had his knees under the table of the archaic Hanley Association for the Prosecution of Felons. Offering rewards for the detection of crime was its original purpose, although, if history were anything to go, Tony did nothing but enjoy sumptuous blowouts.

It was all thanks to Staffordshire's lack of a professional police force in the first half of the nineteenth century. A system of 'constables' was relied upon instead. Had been the way since the Norman Conquest. And when these constables got involved heaven knows where anything might lead.

The story of Hannah Bowers, the 'Sneyd Green Strumpet', sort of illustrates the point. In the village she was known as 'Tanner Hannah' given her virtue could be bought for a sixpence. However not every man pulling up his britches after rumpy-pumpy was prepared to slap coin in her palm. On a February night in 1820, while in the company of five beery beaus, she suffered a triple whammy of unpaid 'connections', a legal term. Thinking herself a professional woman she felt very hard done by and it niggled.

At daybreak she went up the parish constable and reported rape. He knew her reputation was against her. He went and found the quintet and suggested they compensate her with a few quid. Very stupidly they demurred. Quick as a flash they were banged in Stafford Gaol. A trial would await them.

Stubborn Hannah stayed steadfast. Again the chaps were asked to pay up. Last chance. Again they flatly refused. Oh dear, the arrogance that tumbles from principal. Before Mr Justice Richardson, horror of horrors, the prosecution case triumphed. The black triangle was needed. The five were sentence to death.

Mercifully the two beaus without connection were reprieved. The others – William Walklate, William Toft and Daniel Collier – were hanged outside the gaol to the amusement of a large and rowdy crowd.

And the story continued. Hanged for an hour, the three were cut down and dumped on a cart taking them to Hanley for the burial. Following the cart was what the carter described as "almost the whole population". Dead set on a little more fun they became a mob. Every village they passed through was vandalised.

At Stone the anxious carter happened to glance at the corpses. One moved. Daniel Collier. And he was making croaking noises. And only gave up the ghost during the remaining 8 miles to Hanley. Had Daniel survived he would simply have been re-hung. The Law was the Law. But whether it dealt with the vandalism, I found as much trace as I did of Hannah.

When a proper police force did come about, frankly, it was rubbish. Of the two hundred officers originally recruited almost half got the big heave-ho within the first two years.

An alternative was needed. Up sprang associations of panjandrums whose members, rattled by upsurges in crime, offered rewards to anybody reporting crooks to the authorities.

Burslem Association for the Prosecution of Felons, of the same mould as Hanley's, aimed "to bring Offenders of every description to condign punishment".

Both associations dished out justice quickly, if not always justly. Often a thorny murder case would be heard in a couple of hours. Hearsay and assumption were often enough to convict, with all male juries sometimes taking mere minutes to arrive at a verdict.

Behind all this, rewards had a going rate. If a bod reported stealing coal from carts was convicted, the snitch earned £5 5s – about £300 in present money. At £20, reporting a highway robbery was substantially more gainful, the equivalent of over a grand, today.

It's a guesstimate how useful these carrots were. With such good money on offer it's not an unreasonable hunch that many disliked innocents were victims of being 'grassed on'. On the other hand, what if nobody bothered saying anything? For instance, Tony Edwards' bunch of predecessors, had 'a quiet year' reported in *The Staffordshire Sentinel* of 31 January 1880 thus:

*"The Hanley Association for the Prosecution of Felons had had nothing in partic-
ular to do this year except dine – which it did on Thursday in a thoroughly efficient
and satisfactory manner. The fact that the Society has had nobody to prosecute during
the year no more proves that it has existed in vain than the fact that a man's house
has not been burnt down, proves him a fool for having insured it."*

By 1907 the Association's annual banquet competed for the social event of
the Hanley year. Its rival was a custom dating from 1783 described as a
"junketing", and arose because a number of convivial Hanley gentlemen
sulked that Newcastle's civic feast outdid anything Hanley could offer. The
upshot was the 'The Hanley Venison Feast". The merry gents formed a body
called "The Ancient Corporation", and the festive board had a haunch of
venison gifted annually by the Duke of Sutherland. Newcastle got properly
put in its place. Blowouts were warranted and important.

"What happened to Tony?" I asked Rodge.

He furtled for another seed. "Cremated probably. Pneumonia. Fancy
pizza? We can surprise the lovebirds. And before you say anything, Anna
exaggerates. I tired of borsch faster than a fading solstice moon."

Leaving a blackbird mining the Fields for worms we retraced our steps to
Dividy Road where the talk of 'Piccolo's Pizzeria' was Pauline. At seventy-
seven she thought herself a "tough old bird" having put up a successful strug-
gle against a hooded heroin addict who was after her handbag. Like the
boxed Margarita, I'm delighted to confess, Pauline's story was blooming
excellent.

"Tomorrow's Tuesday," said Rodge, "Etruria Locks and Que Sera Sera."

"What will be will be?"

"Absolutely. And what will be will be oatcakes. You have to meet Kay.
She upped-sticked from Dividy Road to make them with her 'owd mon' …
on a canal boat.

"Saturday, I've nothing planned other than the nogger, and you and I
attending the Boothen End. You will be about, won't you?"

"I will be now."

"Excellent. Tony Pulis, our old heroic Welsh wizard manager, is bringing
his Baggies in hope of getting one over Mark Hughes, our new Welsh wizard.
You owe Anna for your ticket, by the way."

"Ah."

"Meanwhile, stop picking at the pizza. Unless you feel Anna and her bog-
snorkeller have devoured each other by now, best not hand them an empty
box."

"One question Rodge. What happened to Anna's little pooch, Jem? The
one we fed chips to at uni."

"She's long buried under bulbs in Anna's mum's garden. Snowdrops,
daffodils, bluebells, and … um … irises. The irises were my idea."

"Oh god, Rodge."

Oatcake, Hoof and Cut

*"The people from the Potteries want to be your
friends and take you to the football and buy
you drinks and tell you jokes."*
Terry Darlington, writer.

Of brick and balanced beauty, the nineteenth century potter's mill at Etruria
Locks ages well. A place of red cog and ratchet, bone and flint was ground by
the turning power of 'Princess', the steam-powered engine. The chimney is
impressively tall.

Small wonder, when this sole existing operational mill of its type was rein-
carnated as Etruria Industrial Museum, famous steeplejack Fred Dibnah
performed the opening ceremony.

Opposite, on a Tuesday, I can vouch a gang of sparrows gather. They
chatter around a small semi-circular sward of grass, a few sparse shrubs, and
one or two trees. And, from the vantage points of James Brindley's head and
theodolite, they survey hopeful of delicately light oatcake scraps.

Fashionable for eighteenth-century style, the great engineer stands stiffly
statuesque where the Trent and Mersey and Caldon Canals have their junction – a busy junction meriting the weekly visit from the 'Oatcake Boat'. And
you know it's the Oatcake Boat that's tied up because of the practical tassly
cushion placed over a towpath path iron stake to help prevent the careless
tripping.

Proper name *Que Sera Sera* it's a functional vessel. The tumblehome – the
inward slope of the upper part of the boat's sides – is business-like. Flowers
grace a hanging bucket. Painted lizards, the inside of the serving hatch. Out
of which passes heritage fare.

The Staffordshire oatcake: floppy, flat but aerated, and about 8 inches across. The Potteries' Poppadom. The Tunstall Tortilla. The original fast food. KFC it ain't. Just oatmeal, whole wheat flour, yeast, milk, water, and the application of heat. Although, melted mature cheddar cheese and best quality crispy bacon, or the gorgeousness of black pudding takes tradition to another level.

Full-figured, cheerful, and apple-ruddy cheeked, Kay Mundy flicks at her peroxide blonde fringe and insists there is a little more to her oatcakes than the basics. Naturally. It's now her livelihood.

In a leap of faith she gave up on her care work job. Her handicraft, she first believed, was the thing. That, and the coot-ripples of the cut. She plunged from Bentilee's Dividy Road into the narrowboat and self-employment before finding small demand for her creative merit.

Oatcakes were Plan B.

Like a Stokie Colonel Sanders the Oatcake Boat's chief cook and captain uses a closely guarded recipe. Her Granny's, she says. Her hubby, Steve, deck hand and general factotum, will tap his nose. Mum's the word.

What could the secret be? Maybe, "Oatcakes must be stirred with one's feet." I quote Mr Todd from the Peter Rabbit TV series rather than Beatrix the Potter.

Kay is a gran herself. To six sprogs! All open to plenty of telly influence. Generations of serious oatcake know-how is potentially in the making.

In derelict Stoke the competition has fallen away. Or, to be more accurate, been demolished. Having served oatcakes through the front window of the Hanley end-of-terrace house in since the 1920s, the 'Hole in the Wall' is the saddest loss. A casualty of city regeneration were lovely people got bluntly told to abandon their rose-coloured terraces. You bugger off, the council said, but oh, have this cash sweetener. Ordinary Victorian character erased – and the world's final traditional oatcake shop, the front room business of Glenn and Sue Fowler, had gone with it.

More than five thousand people signed a petition to save the shop after news of its potential demolition first broke. Course, it didn't do a jot of good.

The city council had rushed to push forward its mouthpiece – a jobsworth. Called Ruth, she was the council's cabinet member for Regeneration. "Waterloo Street is part of a designated clearance area, and we have a statutory responsibility to demolish the few remaining properties in that area." Insensitive jargonising to the detriment of local and visiting mortals, I thought.

Goodness me, I remember the shouts of "Hiya, duck!" and "Do you want brown sauce with that?" floating through Glenn and Sue's Waterloo Street window, along with the smell of sizzling bacon. In 2009, the Hairy Bikers visited the area while filming one of their television series. One half of the bikers, Simon King asked people to sum up Staffordshire in a plate of food. "Everyone said 'oatcake'!" he recalled. "Then the second breath was, 'you've got to go to the Hole in The Wall oatcake shop.'" Heigh ho.

"It's very sad. We're the last oatcake shop that serves out on to the pavement," Glenn Fowler, said on the eve of closure." The people who come here are not just customers, they're friends." Kind-eyed and spectacled, thin as a rake, a blue and white check apron around his waist, he controlled the long steel spatula, flipping and shuffling the oatcake legions on the griddle for thirty years.

The *Guardian* turned up on the last day:

"Customers begin queuing before 6am for their chance to get hold of the shop's last ever oatcakes. By 11am more than 100 people are waiting patiently in the sunshine. As the day progresses the snaking line barely shrinks. The Fowlers say it was like this all last week, and on Friday alone they produced more than 4,000 oatcakes to try to meet demand.

It hasn't been all work: there have also been plenty of presents, cards and flowers. One former Hanley boy, Paul Bamford, 61, catches the 7am train from his home in Hastings to get his final fix of the Fowlers' handmade oatcakes. Placing his order of one filled with double bacon and cheese and four dozen to take away, he says: "It's criminal that it's closing."

In March 2012, bulldozers wreaked their havoc. 'If Hitler had bombed this area, he couldn't have made a bigger mess," somebody commented. Glenn observed it as true. "They've just knocked places down and there's no sign of anything being put up."

Social media became active. "The council should hang their sorry heads in shame," one soul posted online. Glenn and Sue also resorted to the Internet – posting seven hundred sold packets of a dozen oatcakes.

Afterwards, they wept.

Driving past where the shop used to be is nothing but a sea of grass. Interrupted a smidge by an insignificant and desultory cluster of newish housing, the grass reaches as far as the distant hills. It is very nice grass, but you can't eat the scenery.

A thought no doubt held by salivating Dean, a homeless heroin junkie adapted to doorways and bus shelters, when he woozed towards a fill-in van selling "Delicious Filled Oatcakes", 'Oatie Mostons' – a name easily mistaken for a nasty pox – outside Hanley's 'Marks and Sparks'. Dean wheedled for a freebie.

Chef Kevin politely refused point blank. In return he received a facial gobbet of spit. Fair play, Kevin grabbed the nearest thing to hand – a jug of oatcake mix. Dean's noggin got battered to raucous cheers from a gathered crowd. Ah, the people's games. When the police arrived the gloop had set, and it proved an impediment when our miscreant hungrily tried to chew a chunk out of an arresting officer. Grand entertainment. For the spit and chomp attempt Dean received twelve weeks being fed at Her Majesty's pleasure.

From its Etruria summit, the Trent and Mersey canal drops 50 feet. A flight of five, deep, 70-foot long locks assist a narrowboat to not suffer a badly broken nose. Of these, second up is Cockshutts Lock. At this spot the West Coast main line crosses the cut 550 yards from Stoke station.

It is easy for graffiti 'arteests' to get to. And it shows. Spray cans have made an unholy mess of the tatty footbridge and railway bridge paintwork. In the shadow of a dark wall set back from the cut, a grassy bit, and the cobbled towpath, an unassuming and rusted stumpy treasure reads "Shardlow 56" and "Preston Brook 36".

Dating from 1819, it's a milepost cast in Stone. Not the rock, but the place. The place where a murmuration of starlings once held me spellbound. A diving, wheeling cloud of a quarter of a million birds created giant sky shapes in the day dregs before 'moppet'. Stone, the furthest from Stoke the 'Oatcake Boat' tonks, is where local men formed the first jogging club in Europe – tradesmen, shopkeepers, lecturers, a judge, a vicar … and Terry Darlington. The latter is now more synonymous with canals than Brindley.

Terry is the giant, one–eyed septuagenarian narrowboat adventurer and writer who confronts life with his equally adventurous wife Monica and two whinging whippets Jim and Jess.

Three-legged after a duck incident, Jess is the latest family addition. She wasn't around when the veteran trio first caught the world's attention in Terry's book *Narrowdog to Carcassonne* – a 7-miles per hour canal peregrination endured from Stone, which Terry describes as "last twitch of the Pennines before the plains of the Midlands and Cheshire", across the English Channel, and down to Southern France. The follow-up *Narrowboat to Indian River* also lodged in the bestseller lists.

The true heroine of the escapades, Terry takes pains to point out, was the 7-foot wide, 60-foot long *Phyllis May*. Steel shelled, she was "light grey with a white roof, two pots on top and a brass tunnel light, and roses and castles on her back – she was all flowers and fairies."

On 25 November 2009, the *Phyllis May* made the BBC world news headlines for all the wrong reasons.

Terry stoically faced the TV cameras. "It's ironic that the boat's taken us half-way round the world, though tornadoes, hurricanes and alligator-infested waters, then burns to death at its own mooring." A furious blaze at Stone's Canal Cruising boatyard had chanced – the fault of a careless chump doing a flit to London, leaving his boat unsafe. Alongside, the *Phyllis May* was buckled, burnt out end-to- end, and had precious keepsakes charcoaled. Terry and Monica lost all while they sat at home watching the goggle-box.

It was a tragic loss not just to the Darlingtons. The characterful narrowboat had been doted upon, waved to, called out to, and hammered on, by devotees along Terry and Monica's possibly favourite canal stretch – the peaceful, green and leafy pretty patch between Stone and Frandley, where I can vouch for the Kingfisher Café's Staffordshire Yeomanry Pudding. For want of detail: a scrummy pastry tart with an inside of egg custard dolloped onto jam.

First baked during the Boer War by soldiers' wives, the pudding was a treat for their hubbies' homecoming. The Staffordshire Yeomanry itself was a division of the Queen's Own Regiment. Existing from 1794 through to 1973 they have now amalgamated with the Queen's Own Mercian Yeomanry.

Spare a thought for the footie fan. Those in need of a tummy-filler after a Stoke City game faced a dearth of hot treats. Mordantly moored next to the vast corrugated-walled, green-and-cream-lidded, municipal incinerator, the 'Oatcake Boat' furnished the void.

Emerged from the Britannia Stadium Rodge and I queued a distance from the serving hatch amidst a red and white crocodile of mildly disgruntled Stoke City fans. The result wasn't unique in the history of a founding club of the English Football League and second oldest club in the world. Neither was the fretting, worrying, and nails chewed up to elbows. The Potters 0, West Brom 1. Wow-ze-wowza.

But hey, there was still unified affection for Tony Pulis jumpin'-an'-a-screamin' down the touchline in his baseball cap, albeit a blue one.

And anyway, 'Delilah' sounded spine-tinglingly fantastic. What a crowd anthem!

Many an opposition spectator asks why Potters' fans, more than a tenth of the population at each home match, sing it. In truth, I once did, too. But that was during the swansong years of the Victoria Ground. Match days when Stoke striker Lee Chapman got shouted at being "useless as a chocolate teapot", on all but the one occasion. The one when I happened to sit with a mate from Clapham, right in the middle of the away supporters stand. Tottenham was his team.

Lee netted with his floodlit noggin. Leaping from my seat, I punched the air. "YESSSSS!!"

"'Ere," yelled a gruff North Londoner. "'E's supportin' Stoke." My mate, a bag of nervous giggles, thought I was about to die. I was sure I was about to die, too. Better to have stayed standing in the wings where flat-capped and shrunken men prosaically uttered, "Eh, good goal, that" to a Mickey Adams 25-yard humdinger which passed Liverpool legend Bruce Grobbelaar's outstretched leaping salmon flipper. It was a time just beyond the wagging tail-end tip of Stoke's golden era.

The 1970s are still topic in the pubs and on the buses. And entertaining stuff it is to listen to although even a couple of decades ago it had become repetitive. Sublime players such as Gordon Banks, Geoff Hurst, Alan Hudson, and Jimmy Greenhoff honourably wore the stripes. And 1972 brought silverware – the 2-1 League Cup win over Chelsea. To date it's the Potters only trophy of note.

Twice Stoke qualifed for the UEFA Cup. There was no shame losing out to the 'total football' of mighty Ajax on away goals. The Dutch maestros profited from Cruyff and Neeskens. With Kaiserslautern, Stoke only had themselves to blame. Having a player sent off was doltish.

Then a hurricane blew. The roof of the Butler Street stand was peeled back like the lid off a tin of anchovies. The club wasn't insured. Repairs though were mighty essential. Jimmy Greenhoff was sold to Manchester United to pay for them. But ignominy of ignominies before roofers made things hunky-dory Stoke was forced to play a home game on the pitch of local rivals Port Vale. On which note, best get back to 'Delilah'.

Chiefly, a Stokie nicknamed TJ started the bailiwick in the late 1980s when Stoke had a bearded goalie resembling King George the Fifth and a policeman asked Stoke fans to sing without swearing.

Soon the song was given a twist by the Boothen End, becoming the subject of debate from the politically correct. The line "I put my knife in her hand" got given 'erotic' bias, vexing some dads and mums who covered their little darlings' ears.

What made the song unique was the way it was sung. The crowd started it off chanting "TJ! TJ!" That got the maestro on his feet to begin affairs. There followed a deathly hush whilst TJ began the song solo. The rest of the Potters' fans only joined in at the end of each line until they reached "she stood there laughing". After that, the chorus was sung twice. At the end of rousing renditions the home fans all clapped each other. I've never had an iota of a clue why.

When done with full gusto 'Delilah' sounds magnificent. That's probably why Baggies' fans tried and failed to drown it out with a whistling which, in Rodge's opinion, was a sign of heartfelt respect.

In the days of yore the club was known as Stoke Ramblers. Railwaymen not potters made up the team that played its home games on the wintering Victoria cricket pitch. Reason enough, I offer, to translate bowling elevated trajectory 'uptychucks' into the recent Stoke style of play of hoof and hope, and Rory Delap throw-ins.

Believe me, this is not why the traditional Staffordshire stew is called 'Lobby'. Neither past football style nor a cricketer's bowling technique has anything to do with it. Categorically not. Lobby is a leftovers affair – smelly mutton bones and tired veg. Lobbing at arm's length is how the fodder got in the boiling pot. Poorly paid potters were unable to routinely afford fresh food.

Rodge will whinge about 'The Potters' nickname. It's quite wrong, he maintains. Better reflect what Stoke does now as a city. "Perhaps, 'The Warehouse Operatives' or 'The WOs'," he suggested.

"Absolutely. Woes, indeed," I said.

Sean Ruane has witnessed them aplenty. Perfectly noticeable with his outsize red and white striped beard, 2013's 'Fan of the Year' and most recently saluted as the country's 'Ultimate Fan', Sean affectionately known as the 'Hairy Potter' believes the sense of humour of Pots folk is unique.

Well, they are when you bring Potters–potty Neil 'Nello the Clown' Baldwin into the equation. Much happened after he clowned around for Princess Margaret at a royal variety show, falling out of a taxi and being thrown off the back of a fire engine.

The legend Neil became was celebrated in a BAFTA award-winning BBC drama, *Marvellous*. Toby Jones played the part of Neil. And a book that's out should be cherished. At Keele University, Neil Baldwin FC, the club he founded half a century ago, goes from strength to strength.

A prospective fixture list included a game against the All-Party Parliamentary XI.

To throw down the gauntlet and arrange a date, Neil rang the House of Commons, hoping to discuss matters with the Shadow Secretary for Sport, Chris Bryant, and was put through to the shadow cabinet office. The Rt Hon. Harriet Harman is still to reply.

Neil sums up his philosophy on life in his book's very first words when he says:

"These two things I want to tell you at the start.
First, I like to remember the happy things. I put nasty things behind me. And second, you can get things by asking for them. I always do."

C'mon, Harriet, people coaxed, let Neil keep his record.

Spin the time-wheel back to 1991. Neil's indefatigable optimism had him apply for the job as Stoke City manager. Lou Macari beat him to it. But hey, Lou handed Neil the role of kit man – unpaid. Neil's love for the club, then languishing in the third division, was indubitable. Nello the clown became Nello the dressing room jester.

Egos got stung. Striker Martin Carruthers, bragging about his sixty quid silk boxer shorts, was brought down a peg. During a game at Tranmere, Lou persuaded Neil to pinch all the players' underpants – and wear them all under his tracksuit bottoms.

"One by one, the players climbed out of the bath afterwards and panicked because their pants had gone," said Neil. "They thought there was a thief at large with a worrying fetish. Martin was in high spirits because he had scored the winner, but his mood changed when he couldn't find his underwear. I tried to keep a straight face but the other staff were all in on the secret."

Neil peeled off the undies. The pair smooth against Neil's bum cheeks were Martin's.

In a series of away games their kit man donned fancy dress: 'Lord Baldwin of Keele' in top hat and tails at Hartlepool, mutant ninja turtle at Leyton Orient, a chicken at Bournemouth.

A character with a heart of gold was valuable. Lou knew that. And the players themselves? Well, they laughed with Neil, not at him.

"Stoke City didn't pay me, but I did it for love," said Neil. "Lou says I'm his best-ever signing, and he's right." Boastful words and likely true.

Course the players sometimes gave Neil stick. But Neville Southall showed the generous side. When the squad were in Reading ahead of a league game, news came that Neil's mum was taken ill. The former Welsh international cobbled together enough cash for his kit man to grab a taxi back home.

"We were a good team, like Stoke City," Neil says of his late mum.

Sean Ruane believes the same of him and his brother, Michael. "The big man gets emotional sometimes," he says. Remembering his brother's untimely death often stirs him to tears. He laments that Michael "didn't really get to see Stoke in the Premiership". Each year Shaun buys five season tickets despite his family now being only a unit of four. He makes sure there is some- body he wants in that extra seat – not to take his brother's place, but to be "part of the family that we are at Stoke".

He admits being "absolutely staggered" at winning the Ultimate Fan competition. The judges were taken by Sean's thirty-two second video chant- ing "We are Stoke … with a bit of help from Ryan Shawcross and Andy Wilkinson" but it was the Hairy Potter's generosity that swayed them.

Famous now among fellow Stokies, he was christened 'Hairy Potter' by Stoke's Danish goalkeeper Thomas Sørensen. After growing his first mous- tache, Sean had daubed it in Denmark's colours to celebrate 2012's Movem- ber cancer awareness campaign.

These days 'Thommo' is goalie at Australian football's top outfit Melbourne City. A rare selfless socceroo, he recently cycled 4000 kilometres across the US to raise money for a Victoria children's hospital. Small wonder his warm heart fitted in at the Britannia.

As a club Stoke has always been about family and community. They are reasons enough why club chairman Peter Coates – a Stoke lad and a miner's son – has stuck by the club. Indeed, they are why he bought it a second time against his better judgment. His family all thought him daft doing so.

Yet Stoke does draw people to the emotional well of caring. Potent, it will motivate both the circus clown and the mulishly stubborn businessman.

"I thought it would be important for the area if the football club were doing well." said Peter, explaining the rationale for smashing the piggy bank. "Stoke was having a difficult time. It has lost the pot banks and the mining industry. I thought that if Stoke could get in the Premier League it would give the place a lift and would be good for it. I think that that has happened, I am pleased to say."

Jack Butland, Xherdan Shaqiri, Bojan Krkic, and Marko Arnautovic are among other adopted Potters intent on keeping Peter chuffed, periodic blips accepted.

Foot shuffling on the towpath in reading distance of the menu stuck below a serving hatch lizard, and my mouth watering, I was pleased, too.

Then, slowing, another narrowboat – tonk, tonk, tonk. A cheery Brummie shout from the cut: "Cheese and bacon oatcake twice, please!" The glimpse of a dark blue and white scarf.

Rodge gave me sharp nudge. "Look, look. They're Baggies fans."

"Shush. Don't you start," I said.

A thumbs-up from Kay and straightaway came a nudging of sides. Hubby Steve, a Stoke City beanie pulled over his ears and standing on the back counter, mouthed 'whatcha doin'?' at his beloved before cracking a grin.

But a principle's a principle, blooming queue jumpers them West Brom supporters.

"Let us pay homage to the Oatcake

Or Oatcake or woodcake as the old men called them.

The oatcake is not a cake at all really

Not like the fairy cake or the Eccles cake

Not a cake in that way

More of a Potteries Papadum

A sort of Tunstall Tortilla

A Clay Suzette."

Arthur Berry, *Ode to the Oatcake.*

LESSON EIGHT

Horn and Bladder

"Custom is the great guide to human life."
David Hume, Scottish philosopher.

I had better get this right. Horn Dance Day is on a Monday, always a Monday – the one that follows September's first Sunday – as long as that Sunday is after the 4th of the month. Which is as complicated as knowing when it's Easter.

Happily, all was well in Abbots Bromley. The indispensible Terry had got the right day for England's oldest surviving traditional dance. And for that matter the only survivor of its type in Western Europe. Which by its nature carries weight. Thank heavens clouds appeared silk-sack and rainless. After all this is the best place to live in the Midlands – according to the *Sunday Times*.

While the cockerel blinked sleep from its eyes, Terry, casual in horn dance T-shirt, braces holding up his baggy trousers of orange and rust-coloured halves, was at the back of the local butchers inflating a pig's bladder. As vital a part of his jester's paraphernalia as his silly hat.

Men and boys meanwhile gather in the Hurst Chapel, a side wing of St Nicholas' church. Here early light filtered through the arched stained-glass window and onto the customary mediaeval berets, rust waistcoats, and britches. A melodeon wheezed. Fingers wiggled, warming up with exercise.

Ting-ting-ting. A triangle. Ting-ting-ting-ting-TING!

"Ollie! Not now. Save it till we're out the church."

Carefully, using a step ladder and willing pairs of hands, six sets of rein-deer antlers are taken down from their racks – four from the wall below some copper pipes, the other two from either side of the pretty window.

The horns – one or two sets sensibly braced by thin iron rods – wear the patina of ancient relics. A horn fragment carbon dated to 1050. Viking stock, historians say, brought down the River Trent.

Each antler set is attached to a small wood carved reindeer-shaped head. Affixed to the bottom is a stabiliser akin to sawn-off broom handle. It's helpful. The actual weight of horn – energy-sapping heavy – is borne on a dancer's shoulders.

But before anything else, the 'horns' are carried to the altar and reverently placed in a row in front of the communion hassocks. Deft flicks of a multi-coloured feather duster remove the year's clinging cobwebs.

The horns made presentable, the dance can begin. A dance grey-bearded vicar Simon Davis consoles himself is "pagan with a small 'p'".

First mention of the 'Horn Dance' was made in 1226. The church elders reckon it was probably created to celebrate deer hunting rights pledged to villagers in the then nearby Needwood Forest. Ask a local farmer generously handing out pints of ale to the dancers and you'll be told: "nonsense, it's about crop fertility".

Whichever is correct, the Horn Dance is a local family thing, passed down from generation to generation. There is a progression – any young boy handed the triangle hopes one day to become one of the six horn carriers. And it's true of the Bradbury family. Thirty-something horn dancer James says his dad was involved for over forty years, and Ollie, James' small son, was proving adept at triangle bashing.

That used to be the job of fresh-faced David, although that was over twenty years ago. Aged four when trusted with the instrument, he's now nattily cloaked. As the hobby horse his work is to round up all the 'deer'.

A lad armed with a bow took aim. That too is the custom. The hobby horse though faces danger on two fronts. The story goes Maid Marian kills it. And there is a possibility David will die … from laughter. And he won't be alone. Under a footling dishevelled wimple is Johnny, a burly bloke squeezed into a fetching blue dress. A "cock in a frock," he called himself.

A feathered cock crowed. Somewhere fully alert, its timing was immaculate. The hour has arrived to horn dance waywardly through the village. Then out and away past fields where oak trees are singularly outstanding, haystacks square up, and the wind-shivers golden ears of wheat. To Blithfield Hall where Cosy Bagot Jewitt is a tad harassed.

Cosy exudes gentry. Softly well spoken, her bearing is upright – casual but stiff – and her haircut like her blouse is practical. She caters lunch for roughly sixty-five bods. Six horn dancers amass quite an entourage. Her hubby Charles, on top of being the Hall's custodian, is Chief Executive of the Alrewas National Memorial Arboretum. Which means when it comes to horn dancers on the front lawn he can be excused for being otherwise occupied.

A bit of press-ganging and Cosy has local womanly help after she's done the children's school run. Priorities. 'Sickie' taking isn't allowed. Maths, English, and Science are more important than an impressionable child checking out an alarming cross-dresser and six merry lunatics rollicking antlers ... or being bopped by an unhygienic bladder.

Cosy's family maintains a sense of tradition and noblesse oblige. It doesn't matter a fig no longer being wealthy.

Although, in June 2009, she did feel compelled to write a letter to the *Daily Telegraph*:

> SIR – *Our local tooth fairy is seeking advice on how to reply to a letter written this week by our nine-year-old daughter:*
>
> *"Life is getting on, costs are going up. Please, dear kind Tooth Fairy, you cannot buy much for a pound. Can I have just a little more? Lots of love Emma x."*
>
> *Cosy Bagot Jewitt.*

To be fair, that Blithfield Hall exists today is a miracle. One achieved through the trenchant works of the Bagot Goat Society's Chair who passed away, a nonagenarian, in February 2014.

Nancy, Lady Bagot was recognisable for her headscarves and dark glasses. A Sydney-born Australian she was remarkable in a life not just dedicated to small, semi-feral pretty black and white goats, whose horns sweep backwards with minimal lateral twist. The goats surprisingly tolerant of rain are ideally suited to Staffordshire. Small wonder they feature on the Arms of the Barons Bagot.

It was 1946 that Nancy first witnessed the Horn Dancers. She and her husband Caryl the sixth Baron Bagot had recently come to live in the county and the occasion was burnt into her memory:

> *"It was a misty morning. The first thing we heard was the little triangle beating. Then we saw the tips of the horns coming out of the mist from the mill down in the valley and there was nobody else here at all. I felt as though I had gone back in time."*

The hall itself may have that effect on her, too.

Blithfield had fallen into ruin. The only water tap was in the kitchen, a hike from other parts of the Hall. A hip bath sufficed for ablutions. Electricity was unconnected. No heating existed apart from open fires. The roof leaked almost everywhere. And fungus caused dry rot.

Problems Gerald the fifth Baron wasn't of the mind to have anything to do with. Merely a cousin of the fourth Baron, Gerald inherited the title in 1932. Trouble was nobody could initially find him to tell him the news. Eventually he was tracked down training racehorses … near Paris.

His heart never grew to love the run down Staffordshire manor or the local customs. He sold the hall to the South Staffordshire Water Works. The company allowed Gerald to exist parsimoniously in the Hall while it went about building a dam across the little River Blythe. A reservoir would drown the Park.

The Second World War stalled matters.

On VE day Caryl and Nancy pitched up at Blithfield at Gerald's request. The house was full to bursting with heirlooms. Gerald needed his heir Caryl to agree to them being sold.

Sotheby's in London did a roaring trade.

Soon as Gerald croaked in spring 1946 the Water Company sent Caryl and Nancy a letter. Remove the Hall's remaining contents, it read, and hand the house over within three months. Blithfield faced the fate of Drayton Manor. Demolition. Like Peel, potentially like Bagot. It simply would not do. The scales of ineptitude tilted by the Peels had to be balanced.

Having moved into a small hotel in Abbots Bromley the Bagots plotted, hell bent on buying the house back together with thirty manageable acres of gardens for good measure.

Negotiations were tough. At their conclusion Blithfield was again in the Bagot family's possession. The Historic Buildings Council stumped up a grant. And restoration began.

Near the top of the list was Blithfield's Drum Hall, so called because a drum rather than a gong was used to summon the family to meals. The custom caused the heebie-jeebies during the English Civil War. Billeted Cavalier soldiers grabbed halberd and musket thinking the drum roll for a Bagot's luncheon was a call to arms.

The Water Company's letter proved just as rousing and explains why the Horn Dance of 1946 was Nancy's first.

For reasons that are not for here, just after 1959's Horn Dance Caryl sold Blithfield Hall at an open auction held in the 'Shrewsbury Arms' in Rugeley. Nancy bought it for £12,000. Blithfield Hall was hers and hers alone.

When Caryl died two years later the Lordship went to other male relations and Lady Nancy's name changed to Lady Bagot.

In 1986, the Hall was divided into four separate houses. It's the main part that's today owned by the Bagot Jewitt Trust.

Cosy only has a rough idea what time the horn dancers will appear on the drive – probably sometime between twelve and half past.

Forwards and backwards in twin lines they will have danced, and around in graceful circles. Initially down Abbots Bromley's narrow streets, into country lanes, and ducking into farmyards that have provided hospitable ale for hundreds of years.

Not wishing to be too late at the Hall, rules are bent without diluting the tradition. A white van tags along behind the procession giving lifts to the weary, most particularly on the B-road causeway across Blithfield Reservoir. Surely few notice. Anyway, the rare migrant squacco heron or Bonaparte's gull won't tell.

The hoi polloi gather, distanced at the foot of the front lawn. They watch but can go hungry on the field side of the ha-ha – the clever ditch with a wall on its inner side below ground level that forms a boundary without interrupting the Hall's view.

Energy preserved, the Horn Dance reprises with vigour on Blithfield's front lawn.

Their lunch, announced sans drum roll, is earned.

Everybody replete, it's back to the church.

In the descending dark there's exhaustion. After man-hugs, back-slaps, and handshakes, the horns are returned to their rests. For Ollie, at least, it's time for bed. Ting-ting.

Flat Cap and Needle

"Progress is impossible without change, and those who cannot change their minds cannot change anything."
George Bernard Shaw, Nobel Prize and
Oscar-winning playwright.

Convey a brief description of a place and it was probably easier to find. This was how the Anglo-Saxon mind worked, making 'Burwardeslime' par for the course.

Let's break the word down. 'Bur' means a secluded cottage, a bower, if you prefer; 'wardes' is the preposition 'towards'; and 'lime' is the wooded track that once crowned the hilly boundary between Staffordshire and Cheshire. So what Anglo-Saxons aimed for was a lofty umbrageous dwelling within sight of the woods.

Then the name got tampered with.

It was entered into Domesday as Barcardeslim. Subsequent records and charters have it as Borewardesley-lime, Burwardeslem, and Burdeslem. Before any other offers, somebody had the sense for a fait accompli. And Burslem kind of stuck. Till now.

Bear with me.

Writing in 1829, the historian Simeon Shaw mooted Josiah Wedgwood's uncles, John and Thomas, desired something more grandiose than an idyllic country cottage. In *History of the Staffordshire Potteries* Simeon's quill penned: "In 1750, the Brothers erected near their manufactory, (and now in full view of Waterloo Road to Cobridge,) a Dwelling House, so durable, and on so scale of extent, and a stile of magnificence, so far excelling all in the district, that it was called the BIG HOUSE." Literally, I took some words with a pinch of salt.

A sporadic flow of grimy buses and cars splashed in and out of puddles. Urban grottiness. I was as unwilling to become discombobulated searching for evidence of a spectacular stile as I was to let thoughts of Cobridge's infamous druggies and hookers distract me from the main grist of Simeon's nebulous record.

Under the underlined heading **"Wet Burslem day"** I scribbled: "A few brollies, anorak hoods, and turned-up collars about. On its corner and in a bad way stands the 'Big House'. Behind the sash-windows Josiah Wedgwood, potter and philanthropist, ate peas off a knife with a purpose-forged bulge. Georgian table manners! Meanwhile John and Thomas, Josiah's uncles, loved the house so much their potters' wheels turned its likeness into conversation-piece teapots.

"Today, albeit Grade Two listed, the house has problems enough to make Simeon, John, Thomas, and Josiah's jaws go slack. Mortar between the red bricks crumbles and falls, the rear corner has turned and sunk, and there's a massive wall crack. Several years' rainwaters had breached the damp course. The council's fault, Boslemites accuse. The authority, supposedly the building's custodians, had thoughtlessly allowed the pavement to be raised.

"Inside, things are very bad. The oak floorboards are kaput. Mould and toxic spores are a health risk. Nobody wants to fund putting things right. Fingers crossed a museum teapot won't become the house's only tangible memory."

Goody gumdrops, I had filled a couple of Molskine pages.

Across the way, the large triangular traffic island – Market Place – stays saddled with the old Town Hall, a Baroque-roofed and pilastered hulk. Continuing to carry its short-lived 'Ceramica' museum sign, the hall is desolate nowadays. Nuzzled against its backside and equally sad is a contrast influenced by the Russian artist Malevic – the modernist Ceramica Pavilion. Sharp as an arrowhead, the copper roof that kept me dry is supported by a tall, slim needle whose lower end points at the foundations of an historic bottle kiln.

Beneath my feet was the Ivy House factory, Josiah Wedgwood's original potworks. Here, between1759 and 1763, he made his cream ware and rococo pineapple and cauliflower teapots. Stuff that became fashionable.

"We want to know what yer was writing." The curiosity came from a pink haired girl in a quartet of Boslemite youth. The three lads escorting her wore unfashionable 'chav check' Burberry.

"Words of interest about the Mother Town."

"Why?" Again it was the girl.

"I might use them in some form or other in a book, thinking people might be interested."

"You patronising us?" She laughed roughly.

"I meant, I was thinking," I muttered.

They all blatantly had me down as an idiot. A bad neck tattoo in a base-ball cap spoke. "Mate, don't bovver. Nobody gives a fart about Bosnia."

"Nah. My Dad does," said the girl." He comes to watch Port Vale. Proper Valiant fan, my dad…"

Ah Port Vale, Valiants, indeed. Club of the 'Sneyd Green Assassin' Tom Pope – their 'Player of the Year' in both 2013 and 2014. Football magazine *Four Four Two* branded the Vale "Britain's most dysfunctional football club".

It's a standing joke amongst Stoke City followers that Port Vale doesn't exist, that there's no such place.

Many moons ago my finger traced an AA map of England's coastline, searching for Port Vale … to no avail. How could I know that I should have tracked inland along the Trent and Mersey Canal?

A word or two about that waterway. Its digging was agreed bang oppo-site me across the road from Ceramica, in the notorious 'Leopard' pub. Since it began life about 1640, when a couple of cottages were knocked together, the pub had been the 'Savoy of the Midlands'. Josiah Wedgwood's relative Ellen owned it when he 'decided upon' matters that would transform the fortunes of Industrialised England.

Josiah's diary entry of 11 March 1765 mentions his close engineering chum James Brindley whose idea the canal actually was.

"On Friday last," Josiah wrote, "I dined with Mr. Brindley, the Duke of Bridgewater's engineer, after which we had a meeting at the Leopard on the subject of a Navigation from Hull … to Burslem."

Also present at the meeting because he was staying in a room upstairs was the tall, pockmarked, overweight and genial Erasmus Darwin – scientist, botanist, anthropologist, poet and slave trade abolitionist. His book *Zoono-mia* came close to formulating the evolution theory. Odd to think that neither he nor Josiah could have known they were to be Charles Darwin's grandads.

Both men were founder members of the Lunar Society, a dinner club and informal learned society of prominent bods in the Midlands Enlightenment. Industrialists, natural philosophers, and general clever clogs' met regularly between 1765 and 1813 in Birmingham. Not all members were geniuses.

Thomas Day, for instance, was similar to Erasmus in only one respect. That he was from Lichfield. A follower of Rousseau, who philosophised the correct sort of education can create perfection, Thomas conceived an experi-ment to 'create' the perfect wife. He adopted Sabrina a twelve-year old orphan. To provide her with a stoic attitude to life he fired unloaded pistols at her and dropped hot wax on her neck. Disappointed when she screamed he packed her off to boarding school, later to wed one of his friends. Hope-fully a kinder-hearted one.

Anyhow, before 1766 when Josiah cut the canal's first sod and James carried it away in a wheelbarrow Burslem was, at best, a struggling village with back garden bottle kilns.

And there lay the rub. Making a living solely from agriculture had been absolutely unfeasible – far too much clay in the soil. Folk, choosing to eat rather than to breathe fresh air, put the clay to better use: pot making. Convenient outcropping 'tarry coal' fired the kilns.

Until about 1600 'Midlands purple' pottery – very hard, inelegant, and usually of the darkest purple – was fired as sellable jars, jugs, plates, cisterns and chafing dishes. The stuff had to be robust given the market-bound pack-horses, their clinking panniers, and the rutted hoof-stumble track ways. Oodles of smashes, though, just couldn't be helped. The other option, the River Trent, had never been navigable by boat, because of its weirs and falls.

Refined wastages of the likes of Wood and Wedgwood were a devilish nuisance. Yet the sorry trend continued until the godsend of James Brindley's light bulb moment. Which in itself says plenty about James' inconspicuous mum who educated him herself at their Leek home.

When the 'Trent and Mersey' was completed in 1801 it linked Burslem to America via the ports of Liverpool and Hull, and the rest is history. By 1851 the Mother Town's population had swelled to almost twenty thousand – which is a lot in need of daily bread.

Hence, in my Port Vale search I should have moved my finger as far as Middleport.

The Port Vale Flour Mill brought out the hopeless industrial age romantic in me. It's those cast iron columns and beams beside the turbid water's edge. And my early morning goal had been to see the roofless five-storey relic again. Honestly, I dreaded the disrepair I'd find.

I gave public transport a go in getting to Middleport and alighted at Longport Station whose doors sported fresh-ish blue paint. Nobody was about to ask whether it had been splashed on for a royal visit. Notwithstanding a twenty-five minute stomp to the Ceramica Pavilion, it's the closest rail point to Port Vale F.C., providing the exercise to work off match day pies.

I wandered past Longport Methodist church, held my nose at the whiffs from a car body repair shop, weaved around a pair of careering warehouse forklifts, and picked up the towpath. And, instead of the ruinous, I found duplex apartments. Way to go, I thought.

I had caught Middleport's nine million pound facelift that was thanks to Prince Charles. The Prince's Regeneration Trust had kick-started renovations by stepping forward objectively to rescue the fancy Burleigh Pottery brand whose future had looked bleak in 2011. By mid 2014 things were reportedly again hunky-dory in the world when the Prince's chauffeur delivered him for a gander and to open the visitor centre. Regrettably there hadn't been surplus funds to salvage the local chippie.

Way back in the past there was a Port Vale Wharf and a Port Vale House.

However there's nothing existing today to prove it. A chap jogging a muscular lean whippet told me so. That he wore a Stoke City beanie hat didn't make me disbelieve him. Fans of both clubs live cheek by jowl.

The sports historian Simon Inglis remarks Stoke-on-Trent's "the smallest English city to sustain two full-time clubs." Somehow, Port Vale have endured.

Their lowest ebb was in 1907 when the club was kept alive by a local church team who adopted the name. And there've been several homes – ones generally bothered by craters appearing from collapsing mines. Indeed, the Valiants spent more time drifting than they have in a former marl pit off Hamil Road in Burslem. Yes, Vale Park does have clay and a coal seam under the pitch today, but heck, it goes with the territory and Port Vale deserves a 'traditional' home.

A home that in 1944 was the star of a screwball vision dubbed the 'Wembley of the North' – a seventy thousand capacity bobby-dazzler.

But there were uber-snags. Post-war materials for non-essential construction work were very hard to come by. Nor did the club have money. Official bodies were uncooperative. Understandably building progress was slow.

Yet, on 24 August 1950, the gates were opened for a fixture with Newport and thirty thousand and forty-two footie fans witnessed the dawning of a new era. That the ground was still entirely uncovered, and had temporary dressing rooms, was immaterial. And things, sort of, got even better.

On 20 February 1960, Port Vale recorded their record attendance. A capacity fifty thousand crowd cheered as Aston Villa got battled in the FA Cup fifth round.

In everyday terms, however, the 'Wembley of the North' pipedream had all but fizzled out. The club was playing in lower league obscurity. Crowds dropped to below 3000. Vale Park fast deteriorated.

At the end of the '90s, Stoke City fanzine *The Oatcake* blazoned a cartoon, 'Build Your Own Vale Park' – a mashed cardboard box cut up, glued and shaped into a mock-up Valiants' home. Vale Park plumbed the depths. Then the club's saviour arrived.

❖ ❖ ❖

"Does your dad wear a John Rudge flat cap to games? I asked 'Miss Pink'.

"You taking the piss? The bastard's a skinhead."

"That's nice."

Mine was a fair question. It followed a slushy thought of Vale fans, the black and white tenth of the city, continuing to wear flat caps in honour of the "quiet man" John Rudge whose own flat cap was his trademark. Not since the late Sir Stanley Matthews had the spirit of football in Stoke-on-Trent been epitomised by one bloke, a true gent.

John, a Wulfrunian pitching up from ... Torquay in 1979, steered the Valiants from the depths of the old Fourth Division to the First in his nineteen-year reign at Vale Park – a period which saw him clock up eight hundred and forty-three games and three Wembley visits. The latter: the Playoffs against West Brom; Anglo Italian Cup against Genoa; and also a LDV Van Trophy victory.

Although Vale lost against Genoa and the Baggies, the win against Stockport certainly made up for it. They're heady days in the club's history. Days that prompted Sir Alex Ferguson to once say: "Every Port Vale supporter should get down on their knees and thank the Lord for John Rudge."

Yet having written himself into Port Vale folklore, John got the boot after poor league form. The way things ended was savage. The board didn't even express gratitude for his hard work in more than a two-paragraph memo.

The supporters though remained fantastic. After the sacking they arranged a mammoth reception followed by a march from the town centre. And everyone donned a flat cap as a tribute. "There aren't many who could last nineteen years: I just guess I was pretty good at dodging the bullets!" John said.

As an aside, as the '80s became the '90s rivals Stoke City also had a flat cap moment. A short-lived, scoff-worthy piece of merchandising prompted by squeaky-voiced manager Alan Ball's titfer of choice. Both clubs in Division Two hazarded a pair of managerial flat caps popping up for the local derby.

"We'll be up before Christmas," said 'Bally'. It was balderdash. Stoke got relegated as wooden spooners. Gullible supporters buying caps made life very confusing for Vale fans. Ball got sacked and went to Exeter City. A load of unwanted flat caps followed him to EX4.

I know this because his wife Janet tried unsuccessfully to run my once local pub. Boxed-up, the caps were in a bedroom for a short while. Bally still wore his own cap of choice, along with an open neck shirt and a gold medallion. Although large enough to be, it wasn't his World Cup winners' medal. The pub, the Redwood Inn at Uplowman in the Devon-cum-Somerset borderlands, had to close because of a police objection.

Anyway, in 1999, John Rudge made the short trip from Vale Park across to the Britannia Stadium and took up another vacant post: Stoke City's Director of Football. The Potters did ask him to be the manager. He declined. Improper, he said, to go from his sacking at Vale straight into the Stoke role. Course, he was flattered. And he spoke honestly about the affair:

"I didn't intend any revenge on Vale by joining their local rivals. It was just the convenience of the area; my family and I are settled here, it was a quick opportunity to get back into football, and it was right for me at the time.

"I didn't want to move away from Stoke on Trent because the people here are the salt of the earth, I can relate to them, and I will always regard it as my home." Now in his seventies, he's still in the area.

❖ ❖ ❖

I readjusted my thoughts. 'Miss Pink' was talking at me. "... And Robbie Williams bought his girlfriend here, that Nicole Appleton."

"Aha. Robbie's a true Valiant. He's been rumoured to boo in the Wembley of the North," I said. "And the Potteries are in some of his songs. Obviously there's 'Burslem Normals'. And 'Angels', named 2005's best song of the previous twenty-five years of Brit Best Single winners, is about the bright angel up there on top of the Town Hall clock tower."

Actually, the 5-foot tall gilded copper radiance prompted the flow of earlier creative juices. These belonged to the creative who died of typhoid in London on 27 March 1931 and whose ashes are buried in Burslem cemetery – Arnold Bennett. He had thinly disguised Burslem in his *Clayhanger*:

> "On a little hill in the vast valley, was spread out the Indian-red architecture of Bursley – tall chimneys and rounded ovens, schools, the new scarlet market... and rows of little red houses with the amber chimney chimney-pots, and the gold angel of the blackened Town Hall topping the whole.
>
> The sedate reddish browns and reds of the composition, all netted in flowing scarves of smoke, harmonised exquisitely with the chill blues of the chequered sky.
>
> Beauty was achieved, and none saw it."

None saw it but Robbie, it would seem. His mum Jan had a little heart warmer to tell the world. "Robert loved that angel," she said. "He'd stand and stare at it. When he went to bed he'd look at it and say his guardian angel was looking after him. It was lovely." The view Robbie had was from the 'Red Lion' pub right next door to the Big House.

No harm telling the foursome that snippet. "Guess what," I said. "Robbie spent the first three years of life, before his parents Pete and Jan split up, in the 'Red Lion' over there. Pete was the licensee. Course the pub was fairly new then. S'pose it had to be with its 'brutalist' concrete architecture.

"Its first landlord was a relative of the sports commentator Kenneth Wolstenholme. He did that World Cup commentary, 'some people think it's all over – it is now!' at the real Wembley. Fair play that Stokie Nick Hancock chaired 'They Think It's All Over', the telly quiz show."

The buddies began to fidget.

Doggedly, I ploughed on. "The ugly pub you can see replaced the old Red Lion. That got knocked down. A lovely place – Tudor framed and one of the last English pubs to abide by the six-day licence. Think of that! The Sunday Observance Act had been around since seventeen eighty. Used to be chock-a-block of art students and music folkies. The buckled sloping floorboards were said to be really characterful."

"Shut up, Doctor Stoke on Trent!" said the neck tattoo.

"Yeah, shut up!" echoed the other two lads.

"Nn-nn." Surely I hadn't imagined the hint of positivity. I honed in on

'Miss Pink'. "Be honest, how would you describe Burslem?"

"Dunno really…" Several seconds ticked by during which a bus crashed a gear and she got her cogs working. "…Perhaps if the world needs enemas, like me Nan does, here's where they'll shove the gas." The neck tattoo jumped on her ample back and smooched the top of her head. "C'mon Beff," he chivvied. "Let's go to the Saggermakers and chill." And, without a goodbye, off the four skylarked to hearsay's grottiest pub in town.

I was left dissecting failure. Six years after Royal Doulton on Nile Street closed exporting its jobs to the Far East, and I don't mean, Mayfield or Stanshope, Ceramica shut in spring 2011. The City Council had pulled the plug on funding, crying 'foul' at fierce Government austerity cuts. The museum had been open for just eight limp-along years.

Designed to be a unique celebration of the Potteries ceramics industry, it was an exorbitant wasted effort; effort over which some individuals, I'd read, deserved "sectioning". Who could possibly have imagined a hundred thousand pottery nuts a year would visit Burslem? That barely a tenth of the number actually did was still a miracle attributable to Channel 4's *Time Team*.

Coinciding with John Rudge's arrival at Stoke City, the Time Team's entry was a three-day suicide-run with bulldozers, jackhammers, and trowels. Pitted against the Potteries sopping microclimate they had to find Josiah's kiln before construction of the Ceramica Pavilion got underway.

Robin Bush, the team's historian and a chap I knew reasonably well, had put on his favourite cardigan, adjusted his bow tie, and, fortified by a glass of port, sheltered well away from the mud. Front man Tony Robinson just dived in, happy as a clumsy puppy. Excavations went deep. A hideous, low concrete bandstand was expendable, as was the ornate tiled floor of the Victorian meat market below it. Porcelain was found – shards and cracked pots in bucket loads.

And barely above Josiah's stuff was a 'time capsule' of porcelain – a shardruck – of vast amount buried by the Wesley bust man, Enoch Wood. And there was something else he would have hidden if he could – the embarrassment concerning Jonathan Leak. Taught the finer points of pottery by an unsuspecting Enoch, he had married into the family saying, "I do" to Enoch's niece Mary.

Her dowry set Jonathan up with pottery works in Burslem's Commercial Street. But that wasn't enough for him. In cahoots with John Moreton, a former worker of Josiah's, he turned his hands to burglary. The pair, caught with silver swag stolen from the Shelton home of a Mrs Chatterley, was sentenced to hang.

Leniency though prevailed. The sentence was commuted to 'Transportation for Life'. It was a sentence very much in vogue. Well, generally either that or 'Transportation for Seven Years' merely to make the trip feel worth it.

Deserving of the lesser sentence was stealing a pair of shoes, or a pair of cheeses, or a book, or, in the case of Hanley's Thomas Betson, two frocks. The judge deliberated over the misdemeanour of William Bannister. "Ten years," he said. The offence? Nicking "2 quarts of whiskey, and 12 lbs of tea".

On the 18 December 1819, Jonathan and John aboard the brig *Recovery* pitched-up in Sydney, Australia where another potter, Samuel Skinner, set them an example of how to prosper if having the skill and energy.

Interestingly, Samuel had been convicted of nowt. His wife had, however, been transported for shoplifting. Samuel, after loyally accompanying her, began making glazed domestic pottery. Advertising his wares in the *Sydney Gazette* in October 1803, his range included "Flower Pots, Tea-Pots, Cups and Saucers ... Ewers, Chamber Vessels, Cream Jugs, Muggs, Water Jugs ... Children's Tea Sets" as well as plenty of other stuff.

For Jonathan's Mary, it too was a case of for better or for worse. Dutifully, she also crossed the waves.

Her hubby and John were put to work in the Government Pottery. Within a few years each had established a workshop. Jonathan's included three kilns, a house for himself and Mary, and by now their children. And by 1828 he was exporting crockery and ginger beer bottles to Mauritius. Diversifying, he also sent shipments of bricks to Tasmania. They went towards building Launceston.

John meanwhile was an unreformed kleptomaniac. His light fingers earned him six years in a quarry gang before he eked out his remaining days making simple clay pipes in the Surry Hills. Today a Sydney suburb a-buzz with affluent wine bars and gourmet food stores it's the very antithesis of Burslem. Fate deals odd hands.

The *Time Team* hitting on Josiah's kiln meant the architect's plans for the Ceramica Pavilion had to be amended. The needle I leant against was the result and it felt forlornly pointless.

At least for a nearby edifice there's salvation.

Sitting on the corner of Clayhanger Street, a thoroughfare named in honour of Arnold Bennett, is a building acknowledged as crucial to the country's heritage – the Wedgwood Institute. Elaborate brickwork and rich terracotta decoration of its façade crumbles. At risk are moulded figures showing the months of the year and the processes of pottery making. In addition there are mosaics, friezes, and a life-size sculpture of our Josiah. Built in his memory with public raised cash in 1865 it ran courses for the working men of Burslem on science, business, and the arts.

And like at Middleport, the Prince's Regeneration Trust has stepped in with millions worth of restorative sterling. An enterprise hub and centre for start-up businesses is proposed. Let's "create jobs and support businesses in one of the most deprived cities in the UK," it says in its literature. Deprived? Not a very helpful comment. It kind of rubs it in.

A chacking blackbird launched itself from a sorrowful Market Place tree. Oo-er, spooky. How could I overlook being in Molly Leigh's old stomping ground?

A lady of dark credentials, Molly was Burslem's celebrated jally-wow – a witch in Stokie-speak. Born about 1685, she grew up to be an impecunious bad-tempered baggage of a spinster. Her rude cottage at Jack Field on the moors' edge was the antithesis of the Wedgwood Big House. Generations of children have dared each other to run around Molly's Burslem grave three times chanting the rhyme, "Molly Leigh, Molly Leigh, chase me round the apple tree" in reference to the one which grew in her front garden.

Reportedly she was ugly. However this may have just been an unkind reference to a squint that the superstitious called 'the evil-eye'. She earned her living from a few cows whose milk she sold in town. Milk she was constantly accused of watering down. Prominent and unpopular was Molly. But she liked pubs. The Leopard benefitted from her pennies.

Where she really came a cropper was through not attending church. Well, that and having a pet blackbird. It proved her undoing. As a species the blackbird had a bad reputation. It gave a person access to the magic of the otherworld, folk believed. Parson Spencer, Rector of Burslem's Saint John's church, a known drunk, went for the jugular after Molly had quarrelled with him. He branded her a witch and the bird her familiar.

His excuse for doing so relies on 'kim-wam'. He was drinking in a local called 'The Turks Head', when Molly's birdie alighted on the pub sign and soured the beer. No Francis of Assisi, the clergyman took a pot shot, but the feathered friend appeared unruffled after he supposedly hit it.

Next time Molly visited the Leopard she was held by locals in the pub cellar. What went on was kept secret. Yes, she was let go, though the incident gave her cause to give the pub a damned good cursing.

And the story doesn't end on Molly's death in 1746. Interestingly, she was buried St John's churchyard. After Parson Spencer had branded her a witch that's really quite odd. However her spirit refused to rest. Strange things began to happen in town. Some said it was Molly. Others blamed the blackbird. Fewer mentioned pranksters.

Parson Spencer decided on a rummage. Along with a posse of townsfolk he invaded Molly's cottage and found her "sitting in a chair, knitting". The blackbird, loyally guarding 'the nest', was nabbed and the troupe beetled to Molly's grave. The rector summoned clerics from Stoke, Woolstanton and Newcastle and they exhumed the body. A stake was driven through Molly's heart and the chattering blackbird was shut in the coffin. This was then re-aligned north to south from its original east to west. The reason was to stop the spirit wandering. This wasn't a one-off. A similar alignment exists at Rushton church.

Thirst making me brave I scampered across into the Leopard. In for a penny in for a pound, I thought.

Sharon the landlady is a known character. A fire-eater, she also DJs, has similar aplomb on the drums as Animal the Muppet, cooks beautifully despite her Crisp surname, and sprays a synthetic cobweb or two in unloved rooms and corridors for ghost hunters.

And there's plenty of space to be scared rigid. Charles Darwin loaned his cook Mary and his butler Pepper Lees the money to buy the pub in 1850. Before long the Leopard was extended. An extra fifty-seven bedrooms made a total sum of one hundred and two rooms over six floors – abundant nooks and cubbyholes for booing inn spectres.

To spice things up Sharon will happily show off a painting of witch Molly that hangs in the pub function room where, she imparts, a local prostitute was found with her throat cut. A firmly nailed plaque commemorating the canal meeting offers an educational alternative.

Below, the pub cellar has a 1920s' tunnel. Once connected to a brewery on the Ceramica Pavilion site, it allowed for rolled beer barrel deliveries. Nothing sinister. But try telling that to ghost hunters who believe this is Molly's haunt.

Accounts say she's kept company by workhouse children washing their clothes in the pair of rivers running beneath the cellar floor. Should Molly bore of them there's a host of phantoms she can socialise with scattered elsewhere in the building. One arbitrarily flings a horse statuette from its home on a mantelpiece. Allegedly, allegedly, allegedly. And all prime fodder for the TV cameras of *Most Haunted*, whose crew braved the Leopard in 2007.

Their results, I betted myself in the pub bar, were nowt as entertaining as the hoo-ha coming from a tiny digital voice recorder on playback setting. The disparate group huddled over it were rapt. I could barely scribble fast enough:

(Male voice) "We don't know what's down that corridor."

(Group nervous titters)

(Female voice) "Steve, Steve, chuck a stone and see what happens."

(Clomp of stone)

(Silence)

(Female voice again) "Come forward male spirit with some sort of horse attachment!"

(Audible bump)

(Another female voice) "Jane, ask again."

('Jane') "Okay. A male spirit with an attachment to horse of some kind, come forward now!"

Before long a finger hit the off button "Who are you all," I asked, jumping at the opportunity.

A wide-eyed anorak span around in her chair, and replied as if it was bleeding obvious. "We're 'The Brilliant Seeking Spirit Team'."

Of course they were. While ordering a Bushmills did I catch Sharon behind the bar giving her cobweb spray can an extra good shake?

Burwardeslime is not what it used to be. Burslem neither. "Bosnia" tripping from a youthful Boslemite tongue as the place to identify with cannot send anyone, least of all Prince Charles, into a transport of delight.

Heroes and Arrows

*"Darts players are probably a lot fitter than
most footballers in overall body strength."*

Sid Waddell, sports commentator.

Mullygrub is not a rugby term. Staffie for 'to hit', it should be. Sadistically, I'm partial to watching a game of rugger. Anywhere. The muddier the better. Call it the fun factor. And off Stanley Matthews Way, on Trentham Fields, is Longton RUFC. It's not the oldest rugby club in Staffordshire. That honour goes to Stafford RUFC. Longton, though, founded sixty-two years later, in 1935, is reputably now the county's best at handling the oval ball.

The Britannia Stadium's a ten-minute stroll away. Potters fans with nous use the rugby club car park to avoid match-day snarl-ups. Ironically it's been that way since Stoke City garnered the reputation as rugby-playing long-ball merchants. Fans with dosh can dump their helicopter, although none has been seen to date. And bar amenities are open to all. But caution should anyone feel anti-social in defeat.

Fergus is of that traditional Stokie breed who, on noticing a chap sitting quietly by himself sipping a pint while watching the televised sports results, thinks they must be lonely and in need of instant company. Anyway, that's how *I* met him. On that Saturday the Potters were playing away and there had been plenty of room for Milami.

Within a nanosecond he figured I wasn't local. "We used to play our rugby in Dresden," he yawned effectually, leaning back on an adjacent clubhouse chair to enjoy my reaction.

"Really, the little Longton suburb? ... S'pose your aged fly-half once had the legs to bomb it," I replied, a tad too smugly. He came over all deflated. A slurp of ale and wind again caught his buoyant sails. I ignored the burp.

Five minutes, and I had discovered on top of Fergus's egg-chasing addiction he liked ... hydroponics. Gawd, air-pruning pots and grow tents, digital ballasts and CO_2 bags. Basically, plants grown without soil. And incredibly, amongst the pie shop, butchers, and second-hand tut shops, Burslem had a hydroponics store. I was flabbergasted and wondered how on earth I could have missed the delight. I shared with Fergus that I deserved a prize for finding something just as improbable: Burslem Cricket Club.

The ground, Festival Heights, is an oasis where cats harass moles. A grassy sward it's rimmed by leafy trees and wooden slat benches beyond disorderly wheelie bins and modern red brick boxes that blossom the Sky dish. A noticeboard informed me about a forthcoming match. Not of the summer game but of darts. This seemed to interest Fergus.

Ten minutes, and he had me astonished that despite him being a Denstone College old boy he's never heard of the Exmoor 30:30. Fortunately he was more clued-up about the Atlantic lava-lump, Inaccessible Island. The grapevine had broadcast the college's ringing of spectacled petrels and whalebirds, not to mention the Inaccessible rail – which to the ignorant sounds like a Staffie's dig at HS2.

Fergus was able to give a description of the mini footslogger. "Like a thrush losing its tail to a cheese wire," he enlightened.

Twelve minutes, and a topic chanced upon prompted a high-five. Both of us had the privilege once, at different times and for different reasons, of meeting Lord Ashley of Stoke. Or put simply, deaf Jack.

"As politicians go, Jack was ..." Fergus mused for a moment or two, "... the antithesis of Michael Fabricant, Pecksniffian Lichfield's 'metrosexual' of the straw-yellow thatch."

I couldn't possibly disagree. Michael's Commons office, absurdly modelled on the White House Oval Office, is a riot of red, white and blue giant Union Flags, and Stars And Stripes banners. And there is, if to believe Simon Walters, Political Editor of the *Mail on Sunday*, a ukulele on Michael's desk. A former radio equipment salesman, he is a chap who dons pink and blue socks. A chap who "tweeted about having sex with a llama and disowned a Conservative Minister in an expenses scandal and the HS2 rail link. Simultaneously."

Then there was Jack: born and raised in a Widnes slum, labourer, crane driver, first working-class President of the Cambridge Union, BBC radio and TV producer, and, needless to say, MP, as the Honourable member for Stoke-on-Trent South, which includes Longton.

Throughout his political career Jack was always concerned that there were many people too proud to apply for benefits regardless of their hardship. This, he knew, showed the need for diplomacy in handling such delicate issues.

Of his House of Commons battleground, Jack declared: "In no other place can one simultaneously express friendship, hostility, humour, loyalty, kindness, intrigue, fury and boredom – sometimes all in the same day." On the green leather back-benches he demonstrated what could be achieved with no agenda other than a burning desire to help the helpless.

Fergus's wheelchair-bound vaccine-damaged sister saw the benefit. Whereas I, politics dabbling, ring-stained an official looking document with a tea mug, naïve of the calibre of the presence in front of me who tut-tutted and smiled.

Jack was once championed as a possible leader of the Labour party. But that got knocked on the head when he became deaf from the basic eardrum operation that went awfully wrong. The misadventure however made him, to quote Neil Kinnock, "a projectile against the causes, the effects, the privations and deprivations of disabilities".

For three and a half decades, Jack, with his devoted wife Pauline interpreting, was a force to be reckoned with – a campaigner "from his heart to his head and his fingertips" doing his utmost for folk from all walks of life and of all ages, creeds, and cultures.

In 1993, a year after he wrote his autobiography, *Acts of Defiance*, Jack had a cochlear implant. It eased Pauline's load. Albeit what he now discerned wasn't the sound that people with normal hearing heard. Instead, it was a distorted version. "The sensation of sound," he termed it as.

To him the human voice was like "a croaking Dalek with laryngitis". But he could hear things that made lip-reading much easier. It got him pressing for public funds, believing every deaf person who stood to benefit should have one.

His campaign became legendary. And about which he made a thought-provoking comment. "Any attempt to unravel the misunderstanding of disabled people is always welcome. When I lost my hearing and became totally deaf, someone said: 'Jack Ashley's not really deaf, he just can't hear'.

"It seemed to be a ridiculous comment but I later discovered that born-deaf people, who may be without speech, and who rely entirely on sign language, are a distinctive community. They are proud of their history, heritage, and that comment indicated, rightly, that I was not one of them. That is clear in retrospect but it shows how easily misunderstandings can arise."

False impressions or not, Jack was a scrapper. A campaign harnessed in the *Sunday Times* criticising the drug companies over the Thalidomide tragedy had been his starter. Rosaleen Moriarty-Simmonds, a Thalidomide survivor, recently said she and fellow survivors would be "forever indebted to him" for his commitment to securing compensation for her and the other "Thalidomide children".

Other crusades of Jack's followed. Helped were those in the armed forces who were suffering from bullying, and those caught up in nuclear testing.

Hospital and prison officialdoms were made accountable for their grubby kitchens. And grand judges and legal bigwigs were brought to task over their lack of empathy for battered wives.

Jack was driven to right wrongs. Anything trivial was out of the question. His causes, carefully selected, were crucial to parlous people. Ed 'Watch Me Eat A Burger' Miliband felt compelled to say that Jack "gave voice to the voiceless" adding there were "millions of people who are living and will live better lives" because of his campaigning.

When Pauline died of a stroke in 2003 Jack, by now a member of the House of Lords, was bereft. However, supported by his three daughters, and his son-in-law, the BBC presenter and former editor of the *Independent* Andrew Marr, he continued to push unflaggingly and extremely hard-headedly for his aims.

Pneumonia claimed Jack in 2012. He was eighty-nine. Writing Jack's obituary, his parliamentary friend Tam Dalyell noted, "Part of his armoury in combating obdurate ministers was ribaldry and ridicule – done with humour and without malice."

An anonymous tribute posted on the Internet said: "He'll be having a ramp installed on the stairway to heaven." And one of Jack's grandsons announced his grandad had trended on Twitter.

Jack's daughter Jane though summed him up. Her dad was "like a silver bubble rising up in the water that just could not be pushed down". Hear-hear, I thought reflectively, a moment before Fergus, who had begun to squirm, challenged me to game of "arrows" – the Stoke-on-Trent habit, in a boozy kind of way.

Fergus caught the swollen eye of a mate.

His scrums done for the day, a character of cauliflower ears and mighty brawn now played bar prop. Fergus tugged his leaning elbow. "Fancy a three-some, Pete?"

Pete necked a pint with a lemonade splash – his timid attempt at a shandy. "Jeez, totally! Three-O-One? Let's go pepper the lipstick."

Having caught my wary look, Fergus flopped an arm around my shoulder. "Mate, mate, Pete's on about the plonking arrows unerringly into red-coloured treble twenty."

Relative to the past, a dartboard in Longton's smart rugby club was quite up market.

It was a far cry from the places where pianists tended to play for fags rather than cash. Where tinkled ivories had competed with the 'thub' of dart on dartboard since the boom in industry that followed the Second World War – the drinking pubs.

Historically, Longton had many. Some weren't even worthy of the name 'pub'. "Hole" would be more accurate. Take for instance a cul-de-sac today smelling of carbon perfumes and sheared by the A50. Once the fabled Normacot Road, it gained a reputation in the forty years that followed beer being promoted as a healthy alternative to gin in 1830. Loosened Licencing Laws offered opportunity.

In Longton it was grabbed, and ninety-eight new beer houses were opened.

Almost every third house in Normacot Road put a beer barrel in the front room and the householder set up shop. Called 'Selling Out Houses', they weren't pubs but anyone could go and buy whatever they could carry out. They were the first off-licences. And it was claimed if you went down one side of Normacot and had half a pint in each beer house you wouldn't make it back up the other side.

Traditionally serious darts were also in the CIU clubs and working men's clubs.

And darts got a boost through a 1908 court ruling that held it a game of skill rather than chance and could therefore be played without breaking gambling laws.

During the 1930s, what was a traditionally working-class pastime experienced a short-lived upsurge in interest from both gentry and middle classes. And suddenly the pubs were filled with bright young things wanting to take part in the latest craze.

Maurice Gorham in his 1939 study of pubs, *The Local*, ruefully describes how the darts craze meant that "the locals sat in hopeless apathy while young women with blood-red finger-nails threw doubles with hard-boiled charm".

Back in the factories people took darts to work with them. There were dartboards on the shop floor. Everybody on a break had a mug of tea and go at darts.

And the game grew. The World Championship was held at the Jollies Cabaret Club in Longton from 1979 to 1985 when Stoke transformed from being the home of darts to the Mecca of darts.

Rivalries continue right through the Potteries, particularly in the Staffordshire Darts League. "It's this working class mentality," said Pete, whose dad came back after the war and never put his darts away. "The infrastructure's massive. Google 'darts'. It automatically brings up Stoke."

From my own amateur judgment, darts in the county is phenomenal. Players play Monday, Tuesday, right through to Sunday. And it's led to pub players earning more than just a living from the ... sport. Each is a self-made inspiration for the working man. And obviously getting started is fairly simple.

Stokie Adrian 'Jackpot' Lewis, who was the Professional Darts Championship World Champion in both 2012 and 2013, made an insightful comment. "We from Stoke are all gritty determined characters. We always want to win. Stoke's not the richest of communities and darts is a cheap sport. Buy any set of darts and it'll last you years and years. You don't need titanium stems and tungsten tips."

I'm sure 'Jackpot' won't mind me spilling a little footy snippet. He's a

Potters fan. The love of the club began when his granddad took him to his first match. As an occasion it was an unexpected joy. Big surprises can be like that. "We're going conker picking," the old rascal had fibbed straight-faced when they left home.

As for darts, I suppose it's all about practice – working hard. Which I should have done yonks past on my maths. I took Fergus's word that his second attempt at 'double-top' made him victorious.

Teeth gritted, Pete barged back to the bar and asked for a double lemonade top on an ale pint. Nostalgia brimming over, I went to recover Milami. But not before a shake of Fergus's mitt. Hail fellow well met.

LESSON ELEVEN

Bus and Armadillo

"Beauty is in the eye of the beer holder."
Kinky Friedman, author and musician.

In 1227 Hanley was known as 'Hanlih' a name to express a woodland glade. You would be forgiven for imagining grazing deer and playful stoats. But surely not a camel doing whatever camels do. I've a soft spot for a camel. Not the Turkish leaf cigarette. I'm on about a bona fide hump.

It took me long enough to notice Hanley's dromedary. St George's Cross stuck over ribs, whether the camel is rising up or sitting down is hard to tell looking at the frozen moment on the town's coat of arms. Apparently, the beast is in honour of John Ridgeway, Hanley's first mayor.

I heard a whisper it also proved the inspiration for the council to invite camels a few of years ago to a switch-on of Hanley's Christmas lights. Sad an incident on the M6 long delayed their attendance. Those blooming rubber-neckers.

The camel's prominence on the family's shield, the story goes, stems from Ridgeway adopting a camel in honour of Egypt, the ceramic industry's land of origin. Now the camel forms part of the amalgamated six towns logo of Stoke-on-Trent, where hundreds of years of history are, to quote Mike Barnes of *Potteries Eye:* "crammed into one exquisite image that drips with pride."

On the other hand, watching Peter Nicholls' powerful and thought-provoking short film documentary *Stoke's a Ghost Town* on YouTube was dispiriting. But, chin up. The *Daily Mail* headline shouted, "Quid's in!"

As part of the its regeneration wheeze the city council was offering keen first-time buyers run down terrace houses for a pound each. Just so long as a purchaser had a paid job rather than being self-employed, a home in a less desirable neighbourhood would be theirs for a trifle. Initially.

In the small print there's the matter of an additional thirty thousand pound loan repayable over ten years to cover the cost of refurbishment. So homes aren't really a quid, which is a bit misleading.

Advertising hoardings along the side of a street of tired trees further discouraged. "City of Stoke on Trent making Stoke-on-Trent a great working city" was one raising questions on hyphens. "City Sentral" baffled. And there were also some large artist impressions of an uber-cool shopping mall. An interesting afternoon beckoned.

I reminded myself of facts, as I knew them.

The book *Crap Towns Returns: Back by Unpopular Demand* puts the city in the UK's ten worst places to live, joining the likes of Bradford, Coventry and … Gibraltar.

Houses prices are recorded as being more than £100,000 below the national average.

Not officially a city until 1925, the conurbation is nowadays worthy of the moniker 'Broke-on-Trent'. Although the theft of the 'S' from the bus station sign leaving it as 'toke-on-Trent' acknowledges the drugs problem.

The city, a 12-mile straggle, has an area of 36 square miles. It comprises Hanley with the bus station highlight surrounded by the suburbs of Tunstall, Burslem, Fenton, Longton, and Stoke. This last trumpets the train station, and I suffered a tumble in the town hall.

To trip over my graduation gown and fall face-flat at the feet of the University's Chancellor Princess Margaret was humiliating. All I had to do was enter stage right, briefly bow, and walk off stage left. A couple of hundred new graduates managed it with aplomb. Har, har, har, laughed many. On the up side, Her Royal Highness' grin was her widest of the occasion, so impartial observers said. I tried telling Mum and Dad who shared my clammy redness of shame.

But ah, the trains. The six towns that fused long ago were a little world on their own. Connecting to 'civilisation' were the twin lines of the Potteries Loop. Built in the heyday of the railways in the 1860s, the Loop began at Etruria, turning its back on the Manchester-London line to run past Josiah Wedgwood's first factory before looping and twisting through the northern towns. In its heyday there were trains scheduled every twenty minutes. But the Loop died half a century ago. Goods yards got overgrown. The sidings at Hanley were torn up.

The car took over, and there were immediate casualties. Tunstall's family-run Swan Pottery, a harmless old-style potbank catering for the individual things mass production didn't bother with, was an early road kill. Ramshackle and makeshift, it may have been, yet it paid its way supplying red clay to schools for pottery classes. And it made stuff too. Faith was put in a floral painted teapot with a brown horse head spout. Produced by the cavalry load it was ghastly. However, so to was the Swan Pottery's fate. Mule heads from 'the corporation' insisted on demolition. The reason was need for a monstrous roundabout.

The pottery's meek owner Richard Webster was rightly depressed. He had suggested an alternative. Let the "rind abite" be made 20 feet smaller, leaving sufficient room and buildings to carry on while making not a fat lot of difference to the road scheme as a whole. Dimensions went unaltered, horse head spouts became scarce, and pottery vanished off city school curriculums.

Fair to say, roundabouts are important, particularly if you have something that lends itself to being put on one. Like Tunstall's 33-feet tall, stainless steel pyramid-cum-tripod with the image of a bottle oven kiln subtly worked into the sides. Lost, and sure I had last seen the thing somewhere else, I drove around it twice and got honked.

But why blame myself? The *Lonely Planet* describes the Potteries as "a sprawl of industrial townships tied together by flyovers and bypasses."

Even heavy industry is buggered. Gentle service industries and distribution centres hold sway, with Hanley both as the primary commercial 'city centre' hub and home to my friend Mark.

A career in NHS management had changed him little apart from wealth, hair loss, and incipient knackerdom. He still kept his '80s 'Photos' album in the attic. Lead singer Wendy Wu who hailed from across the border in Worcestershire had that affect on one or two Midlanders, and the odd upstart from the South West.

A spirit of adventure had me keen on Mark's suggestion that we meet "by the armadillo." He made it sound as if the bony-plated creature from the Americas crawled out the pavement beside Hanley's new bus station to flash around after dark.

I couldn't help myself laugh down the phone. "Holy moly, how far past the last pit prop on the left did Staffie miners tunnel?"

But in seriousness there it was. Past tense. Miners at a North Yorkshire colliery were already working their final shifts as the closure of their pit brought to an end centuries of deep coal mining in Britain.

How things had changed. For centuries Staffordshire coal had been the fuel of its people. Harking back to the end of the seventeenth century, Celia Fiennes remarked:

"Coales ... are very good and plenty, you might have a load for 3 or 4 shillings brought home yt would serve a poore mans familly ye winter. Its in great pieces and so Cloven burns light so as the poorer sort works by it and so it serves for heate and light: its very shineing Coale all about this Country."

In today's altered state skylarks hover above trees rooted in slag heaps. Newts watch anglers rod-dangle in a furnace pool. And, I've already mentioned, Neil Baldwin is a national celebrity.

"And don't bother sat navving the bus station or you'll likely miss it. It's moved." I can best describe Mark's tone as sarcastic.

"Are we talking old or new bus station?" I asked.

The reply was lengthy. "The old one's a car park, a three hundred and fifty thousand quid car park. The Council had to demolish a perfectly serviceable multi-storey car park to need it. The new car park should have been a three hundred and fifty thousand quid shopping centre. But it's where I suggest you park when you get here. It's squeezed in amongst ghastly dereliction and a haunted, overgrown wilderness of lost memories. But mind the cameras. And I don't mean CCTV. No. Some Scottish director's shooting a zombie movie called *She Who Brings Gifts*. Gemma Arterton and Glenn Close have been spotted warts and all, bruised, bloodied and dishevelled in dirty woolly-pullies sipping coffee and waggling machine guns during a survival journey in a dystopian future. Think of it, a Bond girl in Hanley. Small wonder the Council says it trying to titivate with the place. Some's now pedestrianized, allowing sod all way in for a bloke's car. Less parking, too. Small surprise drivers are going elsewhere. So you'll be able to park fine… So it's the new one. Clear? You'll see for yourself when you hit Potteries Way." I knitted my brow.

And it was almost a sweater when I parked. Winging it has a downside, particularly at roundabouts.

Arriving earlier than predicted, however, I plumped for a nostalgic walkabout. Beyond closed, sorrowful shops, on the stained concrete stairwell leading to a boarded-up restaurant, a scrap of paper was gummed. "Amotz I taking care of myself!" Grand stuff, whoever you are. Or was it a suicide note?

This was the place I once got shooed away from during a university rag week. However, I was wearing a black and yellow duck costume and touted the very politically incorrect student magazine. Taking the piddle out of everyone was considered fair game. Stuffed full of racist, sexist, and ageist jokes I tried vainly flogging copies to browsers emerging from both Cadmans, who offered double discounts on 'radiograms', and Martins 'the 'cut price people' who did likewise on clothes. Successes were few and memorable – a cleaner at Chico's, a seedy nightclub, bought a copy, as did the bus station's shoe repairer, a kind gesture after refusing to re-stitch my come-adrift felt duck's foot.

Back in the present, large zig-zaggy graffiti declared 'Bus Stashuns 4 Weeds'. Stepping over a dandelion clump not a film star was sighted, and I could almost hear the ska trombone of Rico Rodriguez. The Specials single *Ghost Town* had been a '80s cracker grappling urban decay, deindustrialisation, and unemployment, and seems just as pertinent to Hanley now. It would have suited perfectly had Jerry Dammers somehow also included problems of spelling when he wrote the lyrics.

Rejuvenation remains foetal. Although many million of pounds, it's said, remain among the shards of the City Council's smashed piggy bank.

Fingers crossed for Milami and bladder fit to burst, within a couple of minutes I jiggled in front of a sweeping curved roof, V-shaped 'f—k you' columns, and an atrium enclosed by a wrap-around glazed concourse. A belter. Kinder on the eye than the multi-storey car park it replaced, and expensive at £15 million of taxpayers' money, for a glorified bus shelter it looks fantastic.

The design is by Grimshaw, the same architect wallahs who had conceived the Eden Project and deservedly won awards. Safe to say the bubble-like, flora packed, biomes nestling in the former Cornish clay mine draw mortals in millions. But wait at a bus stop in the West Country and one risks rigor mortis, lending me the belief that the Grimshaw experience of public transport was limited.

Now then, firstly, a clay mine is a pit, but certainly not a coal pit. The latter are generally tunnelled, the former aren't. Second, Stokies use buses a lot. And third, only a mere handful of mortals think to visit Hanley. And albeit these include the odd former Bond beauty and a six-time Oscar nominee, doubtless they aren't the sorts to be struggling for a bus. So I kind of twigged the disquiet about the new bus station was inconsequentially local.

Mostly, it's about the size. It causes nose-to-tail congestion being a lot smaller than its predecessor. Either disgorging or taking aboard fares, one hundred and twenty buses an hour fill twenty-two bays facing inwards, like the degrees of a maths protractor. This is designed. To idle around they have to use spaces at a nearby park-and-ride. Such flaws of judgement beggar the question: why oh why didn't Grimshaw have an early natter with the bus drivers?

A related problem is the Staffordshire weather. Daftly, the bus stands are out in the elements. Under dark rain-slugging clouds passengers need either brollies or proficiency at the quick step.

My fancy footwork found the loos, the pissoir costing me 20p. Hum. Urine's whiff already assaults the nostrils from unembarrassed changeless souls peeing up the walls. I turned an eye toward the bus station's Spar shop where booze perhaps unnecessarily taxed wallets and pockets before pickling.

Off-putting too are the obstacles to actually finding the right bus. Yes, there are up-to-the-minute information boards that contain a rolling timetable of bus arrivals and departures, just like a railway station. The pity is they are hidden around the tight corners of the waiting areas. An 'easy to use' interactive touch-screen, whose object is to allow travellers to type in their destination and discover a bus to fit, could have done with several antibacterial alcohol swabs had it been working. And an information point for face-to-face enquiries seemed only to work if there was a mirror in front of the enquirer.

But when all else has failed the technical services assistant director of Stoke-on-Trent City Council has the solution: imprinted memory. "The bus station stands have been re-named from numbers to letters, but so as not to confuse passengers we have decided to keep buses at the stands they would have been at the old station." The fine fellow is reported to have said this with a clear head and without any induced befuddlement, whilst implying there rarely are any visitors hereabouts.

It was the grist for a codger with a hearing aid to chuckle: "Well lad, don't go asking a bus driver if you don't know where you want to go, or what bus you should be catching. They don't seem to like it, and just grunt." Now this partially solved the Grimshaw conundrum. Then the codger began to hum a tune I recognised. I do believe he thought I had asked for 'The Way to Amarillo' rather than the armadillo.

Mark though was right. The new bus station was moved. Backwards. Internally, the whole kaboosh had been unstable. Planners were 'unaware' of coal shafts under the construction site. A poor excuse. They *had* to check the risk. Hanley Deep Pit had the biggest plummet in the North Staffordshire coalfield – one and a half thousand feet. Subterranean diggings are known hazards. Have been for donkey's years. Gawd, they've been in the Potteries psyche ever since December 1903 when a burial service was held round a railed-off hole in Hanley's residential St John Street. Swallowed up hat and all, candle maker Thomas Holland was just out having a stroll. It really is the pits. And they really are connected to the armadillo, which I found thanks to Mark calling: "Livingstone, I presume!"

After affable greetings I truly made a discovery. At 19-feet high the Armadillo is impressive. Yes, it disappoints in its physical resemblance to the animal, the armour though amazes. It's fabricated from three thousand metal disc tags bearing the initials of people who promise to share a story that shamefully few know about. Put simply, the 'Armadillo' is the parish-pump description for 'Unearthed', a monument that celebrates possibly the finest thing Potteries' people have ever done. Summed up in one word: Lidice.

A mining village in former Czechoslovakia, Lidice suffered a ghastly fate from the Nazi's during the Second World War. In June 1942 the men of the community were massacred. Women and children were separated and shoved off to the Ravensbrück concentration camp. The village was burned to the ground, levelled, covered with grass, and erased from maps. The root cause was Hitler's wrath at Czech resistance fighter Jan Kubisch's lobbed grenade culling 'The Blond Beast' SS General Reinhard Heydrich, debatably the cruellest of the Holocaust's arch-instigators. The unquantifiable tragedy was Nazi officialdom's mistaken belief Lidice harboured opposition leaders involved in Heydrich's death. Hitler proclaimed: "Lidice shall die."

In Hanley, Barnett Stross hurled back: "Lidice Shall Live!" He had seen the carnage filmed and broadcast by the Nazis and was deeply affected, as would be any civilised soul. On top of that he was also the caring doctor for the heartbroken community of Czech and Slovak exiles living in Stoke.

Compelled to help he proposed Lidice be reconstructed to commemorate the crime against humanity for evermore. Behind him erupted a groundswell of support to muck in.

Let it be said, Stross, a Jewish Pole born on the cusp of the twentieth century, was a popular figure. Before the creation of Britain's Welfare State he gave free medical care to all and sundry fallen below the breadline. Notwithstanding this, Pottery workers had rated Stross ever since he was an expert witness on their behalf when the ravages of silicosis had prompted a committee of inquiry. His passionate campaign on the matter resulted in government compensation. Not just for silicosis suffers but also for those afflicted by pneumoconiosis.

And Stross's zeal particularly benefitted the miners. Triumphantly he blagged redress for those tortured by job-related lung disease. The miners' respect was earned. It was a matter of course, said their leaders, Stross could count on them, unanimously. This was about solidarity. The dead of Lidice were brother miners.

On a Sunday afternoon in September 1942 three thousand gathered in Hanley's Victoria Hall. And in the presence of Czechoslovak President-in-exile Edvard Beneš, Soviet Ambassador Bogomolov, and Will Lawther, President of the Miners' Federation, the 'Lidice Shall Live' movement was formed. The concluding remarks were Beneš's. "This meeting has made it clear that Lidice has not died: it lives on in the hearts of the people of Stoke-on-Trent at least. From now on, Stoke-on-Trent will live forever in the heart of every Czech citizen."

Getting such a number in the hall was an achievement in itself. I know. Harking back, how hot and crammed it felt with five hundred hoofing it to The Specials.

It was poignant Stross, too, suffered ill luck from the Germans. Presenting a healthy lifestyle lecture on behalf of the Ministry of Food found him caught up in an air raid. A bomb blasted the auditorium and left him badly scarred for life.

Yet by 1947 Stross had become Hanley's Labour MP and Lidice did indeed become a phoenix. The Potteries miners had raised funds of around a million pounds in today's money. They did it with extraordinary generosity, donating one day's pay a week. The Armadillo, three years in the making, cost £100,000 – a tenth of Lidice's total rehab.

This polarises opinion. "I have never seen such a waste of money, can't say more than that," some local grump has said. Other say it flies in the face of Stoke's negative press, and shows, to use the words of Sarah Nadin, an artist involved, "what this great city is all about". Unsurprisingly, where the Armadillo looks to heave itself from the ground has been named Lidice Way.

And Mark was right again. It does flash at night – beautiful blues, including the hue previously adopted, he suggested, by NHS emergency services.

As for the hero, a Lidice survivor Milada Cábová has said: "Barnett Stross was an inspiration, a reassurance that not all people are the same." In Stoke-on-Trent he stays remembered in Little Chell, the city's northern outpost, where Barnett Grove and Stross Avenue exist in his honour. Fitting, I guess. John Marius Wilson's *Grander Imperial Gazetteer of England and Wales*, amassed between 1870 and 1872 cited the natives as "chiefly colliers and potterers." Potterers! And, actually, the mining connection was massive. On the eastern outskirts is the moribund Chatterley Whitfield Colliery. Once the Potteries largest mine, in 1937 it became the first British colliery to produce a million tons of saleable coal in a year.

The light bulb moment that Little Chell manor was owned by the Sneyds well into the 1800s triggered me to badger Mark for any Keele news. His reply was topical. Some of the Uni's music students had had their original compositions featured in a documentary film called *Lidice – A Light Across The Sea*. It's been well made by a couple of Stokies. And Stoke City have helped make people aware of it."

"The football club have?"

"Absolutely. The chairman, Peter Coates, got involved, offered the dosh to help finish the film, and then had it featured in a Saturday match programme. You can watch the thing. It's up on YouTube. "

"Good on everyone," I said.

"Yeah, but pity there's little light on 'Sentral'," he countered. "You'll cringe me telling you I'm spelling that with an 'S'." My brow knitted again. I remembered the hoardings. Maybe I also had the solution where the bus station's nicked 'S' went.

"Totally flummoxed me, too," Mark added observantly.

"Silly name for Hanley's shopping centre should it ever get a revamp and cast shadows over the Armadillo."

'Sentral' was proposed by a creative branding agency. The reason? It said: "The use of the 'S' in 'Sentral' reflects the very nature of the (shopping centre) scheme, Stoke-on-Trent as central, while also giving it stand out quality... and it links to the local newspaper the *Sentinel*."

Blooming Nora.

BBC Radio Stoke was inundated with unhappy callers. "It makes us look like the people in Stoke are thick," said one. "Sentral is not a word," commented a pedant. Destination Staffordshire put their oar in. "People don't have a problem with Vodafone being spelt without a 'ph'. Nobody thinks they are stupid." A former elected mayor cut through the blather: "What matters is what the shopping centre looks like." A word vacuum followed, and the Council lost patience with development partners.

"Ballsed-up cock-up is putting it mildly," said Mark. "And I thought the NHS had problems. Three hundred and fifty million quid was set aside, and nothing. Everything's fallen through."

To nitpick Mark wasn't altogether right. From Council spending, a done deal with only lip service paid to local opinion, arose the newly opened 'Rubik's Cube' – a looming primary colour patchwork, officially named the 'Smithfield Centre' targeted for civic service.

Grumbles have wormed out. A space that's unneeded and unfillable they say. Truth is it's hard to justify anything artistic or appealing about the gaudiness. But I speak as one who likes matt white. And the cheese-parer in me cannot countenance the cost. Beleaguered by concrete gremlins, the edifice, paid for by closing old folks' homes, community centres, and getting rid of lollipop ladies, burned £55 million.

Crikey, with the figures totted up I was glad 'Man of Fire' was innocent of wrong. Good old 'MOF's' been around since 1963. Londoner David Wynne's thin, 35-foot aluminium spiky-man was inspired by the kilns that dominated the city. Outshining his Debenhams host atop the shop's entrance, to many Stokies mistaking flames for icicles he's lovable 'Jack Frost' – none having binoculars handy to read the sculpture's inscription: 'Fire is at the root of all things visible and invisible'.

"Fiery Man's as fine a landmark as Webberley's Bookshop," I said.

Mark shook his head, despairing." 'Fraid old Fiery's gonna be the last character standing. Webberley's is closing down. Sad. Been here a hundred years. Last nail in Hanley's coffin, I reckon. You can't blame the owners wanting slippers. They say the shop's unviable despite Staffs Uni on the doorstep. Nobody else sensible's going to give it a go. I'll miss ducking run-along-a-ding-ding life for a thumb and dip. Least I've got a Kindle."

Heigh ho. The oasis was unforgettable, a claustrophobia amongst creaky bookshelves. I'd thought it organic and it had sucked me in. The Knut Hamsun and Hermann Hesse novels I'd once bought were still somewhere at home. And the customer service. So civilised. Fine as anything in swanky anywhere. But the building… Oh, the imperious building.

I became fatalistic of Hanley damp and roosting pigeons, hoping upon hope all the windows were shut tight when the doors were finally padlocked. Rot would lead to the bricks and mortar being judged unsafe. And hang preservation orders. Blink, and wrecking balls will ensure lurid colour-clad concrete rises in Webberley's corner space. Or perhaps it was just my blood sugar level talking.

"Shift yerself," Mark chivvied, " stop staring at nothing. Let's go find a drink." What a mind reader.

As it happened, outside the Potteries Museum and Art Gallery, drink found us.

Its imbiber leaned rat-arsed against the brick plinth supporting the designer of the Spitfire. Of which example RW388 rests inside the Gallery. As a wartime memorial it's the antithesis of the Armadillo. The plane's life wasn't heroic. Donated in a frail state to the City of Stoke-on-Trent in 1969 it was formerly delivered new to RAF 667 Squadron in August 1945 for short-lived and humdrum gun-laying practice. Four months before the squadron was disbanded.

And the Spitfire notwithstanding, preventing the drunk mundanely splatting face flat was, however, reason enough to warrant plonking Reginald J. Mitchell's bronze statue further from his semi-detached Butt Lane birthplace in Talke than to the pub nearby to us bearing his name. The sort of establishment shy R.J.M. wouldn't have been seen dead in.

Aloof, dapper in jacket and tie, his face wears an intriguing self-conscious smile. I put this down to him being the 2003 BBC Online, TV, and radio vote surprise pick as the 'Greatest Midlander'. A cold pipe occupying his right hand is proof positive his dreams of death by beauty were anything but fanciful. And evidenced by the closed book held in his left, that he was a genius hasn't been opened to debate.

A moot point was whether the drunk heaving himself toward Mark and me was going to make it. A pigeon landing on Reginald's head cooed.

"You both can run Hanley down much as you like," rasped the drunk. "I'm on the scene. We're the most friendly people in the country. Brilliant innit. We look after each other, see. Yesterday dinnertime's proof. Me and Frank – who's not here 'cos he's crashed in Hanley park – were having a fag outside 'Spoons' and had the shock of our lives. Young Brasso shows up. He's been released. We hadn't seen him for years and he treated us both to two beers each and a pie each as well. He a good lad that one. But he still carries a torch for Big Mandy. We keep telling him she don't swing that way and if he pesters her she will give him a knuckle sandwich."

I asked if his pie was better for the teeth than a BM sandwich. Instead of replying our new friend chose to turn his back, preferring R.J.M.'s company.

"Mark, fancy a gander at the 'Mitchell'?" I asked.

"You do realise it's the Wetherspoons our nameless friend's on about? They start drinking there at eight o'clock in the morning."

'C'mon. Be brave and mingle. I've got the tummy rumbles."

In tentative agreement to that, off we rambled to Tontine Street where wind-gusted litter danced in shadow. A thin adroit busker beat a homemade metal 'cushion' with a pair of pad-ended sticks outside the African Caribbean Food and Hair Product cash and carry. The sound was incongruously cowbells rather than calypso. But hey, rooted half way up the wall of the perished Harvey's pub on the corner, a butterfly bush oscillated.

The 'Reginald Mitchell' is in Tontine Market, originally built for meat sales. Within its Doric entranced façade the forebears of Potteries' folk chancing an escape to a better life in the New World once drew lots for tickets. Today getting in across the Pond is a lottery of an altogether different nature. American airport scanners and sniffer dogs won't let an oatcake through.

Sitting in the drab dark of the pub's upstairs, away from the dipsomaniac diehards, the topic of food brought a sigh from Mark. He perused the food stained paper menu over a cheap pint while I preoccupied myself with a tissue wiping at the faint lipstick stain on my cider glass' rim. "Go for the pulled pork bap," I suggested. "Don't go with the fish and chips, we're a long way from the sea."

And despite barmaid Rachel trying to work cheery magic he regretted his stubbornness.

I smacked my head. "Of course!" The pyramid thingy on the roundabout – that was on Reginald Mitchell Way. Mystery solved. It used to be where 'Golden' now is. I felt a whole deal better.

"Hit yourself any harder, Charles, and I'll be dialling nine-nine-nine."

Memory jangled. "Remember the old ambulance and the dawn of the severed hand?" I asked.

Mark's mouth went slack before tightening to a grimace. "Rudyard Lake?"

"Hmm-hmm, 1982," I affirmed, chuckling at his power of recall.

There was once a time – the Victorian and Edwardian eras – when the 2½-mile-long stretch of water attracted twenty thousand trippers a day, come sun or snow. The Blackpool of the Potteries and the Geneva of England were the lake's twin tags. Celebrities came. Shops and factories in Leek closed for the occasions. African-American Carlos Trower, "The African Blondin", suspended some hundred feet above the ripples, tightrope-walked across the lake to oohs and ahs from packed stands. Captain Matthew Webb – the first man to swim the English Channel – top billed at a grand "aquatic fête".

Myself, Mark, Ejaz, and his Sikh friend Sirindar encountered eerie silence. We had the lakeshore to ourselves. Getting there had been jerky. Sirindar's rickety NHS ambulance, bought on the cheap, was our student accommodation for the short summer night. There were stretchers. Whiskey was drunk. Tales were exchanged. Sirindar became comatose. The hours whiled away. I finger-plucked the tune from *Tales of the Riverbank* on my Spanish guitar maybe too repetitively. "I am just going outside and may be some time," said Mark, doing a Captain Oates impression.

The squawk Ejaz and I heard was something awful. We both scrambled. I grabbed for my pixie boots. Sirindar sat bolt upright snagging his turban. He became to resemble a loosely swathed pharaoh's mummy, his hair as long as Rapunzel's. I recall the apparition as astonishing.

Mark was found shaking in dawn's first light. He pointed at a drowned rubber glove.

Still to catch up with Ejaz I decided to give Hanley another day come the morrow.

Shocks and Paint Pot

"It's cool to be different and just be who
you are and shock people in a good way."
Brendon Urie, American singer-songwriter.

I was up with the late singing blackbird.

The south side of the wide A5008 road divide, my Moleskine reminded, was for the afternoon. The scribble said: "Meet Ejaz outside new mosque. 2.30. Ask if perfected strawberry yoghurt chicken." A third class degree in computer studies had served Ejaz famously; the settlement after a painful divorce not so much.

The north side having the City Centre and with the morning to fill I relied on whimsy.

I wondered if the legendary 'Electric Bar' had gone. Out of rare unhelpfulness Mark hadn't a clue if it had or not. Pubs had been knocked down for fun. Climbing Huntbach Street out of Hanley for nostalgia's sake, I shoved Milami into second gear and was unnecessarily primed to wrench into first before reaching the hilltop. Small cars had improved since the 1980s when my student-crammed Beetle delivering us to a 'current lesson' faltered to the summit.

This, the highest point for miles, was used to good advantage for ages. There was a windmill here in the early decades of the nineteenth century when life was pastoral and remote. A cartographer marked it as one of the highest market towns in England having measured it being almost 600 feet above sea level. Obviously the mill was higher still. A chap called William Dodd got his hands on it in 1848 and converted it into an observatory equipped with telescopes and a camera obscura, the optical gizmo which lead to photography.

An eccentric, Dodd viewed his acquisition as home and served summertime teas to astronomically-minded guests. Cruising past I noticed the observatory is now a meeting place for community learning and support based activities. I pondered if anyone gave the inspiration that it had been the place for stars.

More wonderful was the Electric Bar. The only pub left standing in the neighbourhood, there it was in green livery existing under its real name, the Queen's Arms. Here Mark, Ejaz, and myself had learned from landlord George Gwilt how the working class pub got its sobriquet. It was from something shocking.

Pre Second World War, a hand and foot rail had been fastened to the bar and connected to an electric supply. The purpose was to warm the hands and feet of workers when they drank at the bar counter. However the rails weren't turned on until just after last orders. When the licensee switched on the power everybody leaning on the rail got zapped. A draconian way, indeed, of underlining "time gentlemen please".

Reputedly, American forces based at Keele during the war considered it a proper laugh. Herds of them journeyed to the attraction. When it transpired the bar rails had been wired it up wrong in the first place they were removed in 1954. Miraculously nobody got killed beforehand.

However, taking the biscuit in foot warming method remained the 'Pig and Whistle' in Longton's Flint Street. Branderick the landlord scattered hot coals around the customers' feet to scare them off if he felt they weren't spending enough on ale.

Curiosity sated, I descended the hill back into Piccadilly where the tower clock said nine-fifteen, large red '50% off' ladies designer wear posters persisted, and time was killed by groups of multi-cultural youth listless outside empty shops. Breakfast at the smart looking Café Toffs appealed. No pobs or fried frogs were guaranteed. Anyway, the signage had snared me. 'Coffee', 'Sandwiches', 'Cappuccino', 'Panini'. I was intrigued. Had I happened upon a new Potteries custom? A posh cappuccino based on chicory, perhaps.

Instinct was to ask straight away upon opening the door. Instead I heeded being on CCTV. And the kindly smile taking my order meant my question could wait.

Going by my taste buds the sample cappuccino was definitely made with coffee. Gesticulating that I had time to finish it leisurely before a scrummy full English arrived would have been rich.

Daniella, the café's owner, pounces on facts. She makes sure they are right. The camera spy is her aid for a brusque response to mean comments, she feels, get unfairly posted on the likes of Trip Advisor.

A stroppy bloke sat at a pavement table with his pooch is an example.

Toast gone cold ahead of hot eggs and bacon was the problem. Daniella was driven onto the offensive. "In respect to your statement the breakfast was served 'a few minutes' after the toast, I can say it was ONLY 01.48 minutes." The cooling Staffordshire air doesn't appear as an issue. Which is as odd as coffee and cappuccino having grounds to be different.

It was only afterwards whilst admiring the gorgeously renovated Bethesda Chapel that I chided myself for not asking Daniella whether her café attracted the custom of the Honourable Tristram Hunt, a regular face on the telly and whose articles grace the *Guardian* and *Observer*. A notable toff, the MP for Stoke-on-Trent Central, hitherto Hanley, is a gentleman proven to have controversial opinion.

A commercially successful historian specialising in Victorian urban history, Tristram was moved to call Bethesda Chapel the "Galleon of the Potteries" in comparison to Ely Cathedral being the "Ship of the Fens". Quite inappropriate, I thought, putting my oar in. The Fens are blessed with waters aplenty. Hanley offers the Caldon Canal. Bethesda would be a tight squeeze after one hell of a slipway from Albion Street. I mean golly, this chapel's humungus. Built in Italianate style with a stuccoed facade it's one of the most ornate urban Methodist chapels anywhere. Up to three thousand worshippers used to pass between the fluted Corinthian columns to congregate for a service.

Greater numbers flock to Intu Potteries, which is the modern marketing-speak for Hanley's multi-level indoor shopping centre. And somewhere on the fourth floor was Jabez. I wanted to see him for reasons of pathos. Thanks to my visit to Wild John I knew what Jabez looked like in a crowd. There was just about time before risking a parking ticket.

Wilfred Bloor had put Jabez' cheery stomping ground between Audley and Silverdale. It's a small area. In the middle of which is Halmersend. And Wilfred would have known it. Perhaps the gentle comedy of the books was a way of coping with tragedy and as balm to the local people.

Including a rescue worker, a hundred and fifty six men died at Halmersend in 1918. The Minnie Pit disaster was Staffordshire's worst mining accident. Families had lost men on the Western Front men and now at home. And it took twelve months to recover all the bodies from tunnels and shafts.

The cause was firedamp – the name given to a number of flammable gases, especially methane. What happened at Minnie Pit was "an exploding bag of foulness". In others words, a gas pocket under pressure. And, putting its high profitability aside, Minnie was known to be dangerous. What kind of character one can ask was the mine owner's daughter after whom the pit took its name? The committee of enquiry didn't blame anyone in particular. The common term 'brave miners' was apt.

Among the dead was Samuel Richardson. He was found with his bible beside him. As well as a miner he had also been a prominent member of the local Methodist chapel. During the Miner's Crisis in 1921 his bible was auctioned in London to provide relief for the striking miners. Samuel's son bought the holy book back for a heart-rending guinea.

Only in the early 1980s did the National Coal Board and the local council erect a memorial on the site of the disaster.

The mural of Potteries' yesterdays is also a memorial of sorts – one that prettifies the area from the shopping centre's car parks to the entrance walkways. It's a few decades old now. Pity two hulking pay-station cash machines have fashioned a thoughtless mask. Modern priorities, I suppose, are put above awakening all comers to how ruddy special the area is.

Here in vividness the 'Hole in the Wall', the last oatcake shop; Captain Smith alone on the bridge of the sinking *Titanic*; the loading of a bottle oven; Sir Stanley Matthews bamboozling the opposition; Trentham Colliery's winding gear grinding at the pithead; and, in contrast, swans gracing the moat of Ford Green Hall. Not only was Jabez unmistakable he was also, at my guess, the only fictional character.

The rest of the content I had to research. Hidden by the coin-gobbling contraptions are Arnold Bennett, a gas-lit street, reeking chimneys, slag heaps, and a boozy bloke wheelbarrowed home by a Methodist minister.

At eighty-two years old, his hair and goatee beard snow white, the artist David Light still leaves his Norton home for work. Colourful brush strokes will be scrutinised through wire-rimmed spectacles and his smock unconsciously paint-splotched. Lately a Stoke pub had his sober attention. Beforehand he commented: "I have always been as accurate as I can be with my work, I like the murals to show some sort of chronological order."

Not so at 'Ye Olde Bull and Bush' where the landlord wanted "a jolly mix of everything." Although here again are David's favourites, Captain Smith lies on the floor beneath a table at which Charles Darwin chats to Sir Stan while Wedgwood listens in, undistracted by the first Minton bone china piece being produced. Really, its not too far fetched. Ghosts have time to be sociable.

Quite honestly though, David is a polymath, a North Staffie to his core, and never too demonstrative. A witness to how the world works he had many other arrows in his quiver of talent, from teaching Ghurkas in Malaya to proficiency with an array of musical instruments. Of the Intu mural he's gone on record to say: "the pictures accurately depict the way we were. In view of the decline of industrial Stoke-on-Trent, I really think it's a shame to cover them up." Too right. Poignantly, a verse of his poetry rather sums things up:

> "Parents and grandparents, our children's children too
> Must realise with wondering eyes that they are nothing new
> The past is going, going, gone."

This isn't exaggeration. Generations of David's family worked in the pottery industry.

However there abide kiln glows hot enough to fire the imagination of another octogenarian mural painter.

Pride of place at the popular Emma Bridgewater factory is a picture of Stoke-on-Trent as it has never been seen before, as it never was, and never will be. Using whopping artistic licence – 8 feet by 12 feet of it – Emma's father-in-law Peter Rice has depicted the Potteries as ... the Bahamas. It was his son's idea Peter insists.

Set amongst sun-kissed palm trees is the Wedgwood factory, Spode, Burslem School of Art, Longport Wharf and Mow Cop Castle. As for the clear blue canal running the breadth of the picture, I fancy the Caldon had never looked so inviting.

Peter defended himself against incredulous journos. "People have this misconception that Stoke-on-Trent is a dull and dirty place but we wanted to show them that in fact, it is lovely and beautiful." Bless. A renowned theatre designer, Peter has for six decades designed sets and costumes for plays, operas and ballets including the Royal Opera, and Glyndebourne. How well he must know people dote on escapism.

Ejaz had been doing it forever. And I found him waiting at the point made obvious by a prominent jumbo green dome at the north end of Hanley Park. In the community of prayer mats, and hijabs the Regent Road mosque really is huge. Possibly it's the biggest place of worship in North Staffordshire.

The ledger opened around the millennium. Currently the bill pushes towards £2.5 million. A collection bucket is put at the back after prayers. There have been positives. The hill of land to build on came cheap. And, I fathomed, vehement local umbrage over the Council's tiddly charge for the lease had largely subsided. A peppercorn though is a peppercorn – even one of £1. I recall such riches buying me a damn fine pint of Pedigree. Matters became more politic, however, when an additional £70,000 was forked out for the mosque's land.

Although not a Muslim himself Ejaz has friends who are. He introduced me to Baz, a Sunni, whose beard has the same abundant growth as the one attached to England cricket star Moeen Ali.

I asked Baz how the money for the mosque, bucket apart, had been raised. "Door to door, week in week out for years. Around the country hundreds of mosques have also been fundraising in a similar way."

To quote a few facts, alone in Stoke-on-Trent there are fifteen mosques. Burton-on-Trent has four. And both Stafford and Lichfield have one apiece. At the 2001 census there were 7658 Muslims in Stoke-on-Trent and 6081 in the rest of Staffordshire, with a total of 13,739 making up 1.3% of the population. To makes things tidy, 62.9%, or 3823, of the Muslims in the rest of Staffordshire are from Burton-upon-Trent.

"How many come here to pray nightly, and how much does each one donate?" I asked, unheeding of Ejaz's 'shush' at my impudence.

Baz chuckled. "Three or four hundred come. And my own mosque's not far away. There we always have a couple of hundred. A tenner is what's encouraged. Then there are the phone-ins."

"Phone-ins?"

"Yeah, on Sky TV. Over the years there've been dozens of fundraising phone-ins on Islamic channels. And you cannot ignore the usefulness of Chanda."

"Which is?"

"Financial contributions – money that's collected in all sorts of ways by proactive Muslims travelling to cities all across England. It's done very nicely. So after ages and ages and thousands upon thousands giving money it leads to..." Baz gave a nonchalant wave towards the new mosque. "Course we've had the *problem*," he added.

"What? The bad press? Daesh? Niqabs?" I asked, stopping myself from counting anything thing else off with my fingers.

"Arson."

"Cripes."

"The mosque had a fire on the ground floor. A pair of Stokies connected a pipe to a live gas main and fed it into the building's first floor, lit a match and phoomph. I heard it was retaliation for some of our extremist idiots burning remembrance poppies. What can we do?"

"Keep trying to be kind. I can't forget having to stand sardine fashion on the London tube while feeling extremely unwell. A Muslim chap offered me his seat."

"That's as it should be," said Baz. "Here, we urge people from all groups to come along and see what we are doing. Guys like my Indian friend here." Ejaz waggled his head making Baz laugh, "I love him when he does that." Silent for a moment, he added: "I help out in the community centre, which honestly is open to everyone."

Leaving Baz to make mugs of iffy instant coffee I asked Ejaz if he ever thought of leaving the Potteries. "Only in the twilight world between wake-fulness and sleep," he replied. Yes, he had travelled. Gothenburg, Glasgow, Silicon Valley, Leeds. But his pad was where, he believed, people were the "friendliest".

I told him somebody had said the same thing only yesterday. Then it dawned on me: local warmth gave Baz's coffee a proper chance of becoming popular.

LESSON THIRTEEN

Parrot and Void

*"If some great catastrophe is not announced every morning,
we feel a certain void. Nothing in the paper today, we sigh."*
Lord Acton, historian, politician and writer.

Duty called to install a cash machine, Ejaz bade me farewell. Anyway, he didn't fancy a nostalgic look at Arthur Street our long ago off-campus student home in Silverdale. Despite his present "shit storm of a life" he hadn't hit the necessary depths for a return to the scene of 'Ghandi's Revenge'.

The subject of a cringeworthy story, Ghandi had been Ejaz's adopted scrawny pet parrot until it accusingly squawked, "Curry!" and stiffly hit the bottom of its cage. Wild John decided on a wake and proposed an alcoholic concoction fit for deep mourning. Among his bottles was a notable pair: 'la fée verte', absinthe, and, the joy of pomegranates, grenadine. The vote to christen the blend 'Ghandi's Revenge' was carried unanimously. What followed wasn't pretty. Not for no one. The vomiting was gut-wrenchingly noisy and launched projectile violent blindly from the upstairs back room into the night. The coalbunker suffered. As did neighbour Alan's neighbourliness. "Filthy creatures!" he yelled at us. Wild John unhelpfully giggled, "rich coming from a miner".

Come daylight Alan tapped on the back door, stuck his head in, grimaced at the assault on his nose, and through gritted dentures informed us limploppets of no more signings-in to darts evenings at his Working Men's Club and wished he could emigrate.

I reminded myself Silverdale miners had actually done so. The most notable was Sir Joseph Cook. Of course, he wasn't a knight when, in 1885, he and his new bride Mary paid thirty-two quid for a pair of one way tickets to Australia aboard the *John Elder*.

At twenty-five his age was on the cusp. Typically, about forty per cent of miners were younger. The early twenties, when earning power was at its height, was the age group proportionately most attracted to nineteenth century emigration. So Joseph certainly wasn't a trendsetter. Between 1854 and 1902 almost a hundred-and-ninety-one thousand miners of all kinds emigrated from Blighty. Over half went to the United States, but almost twenty-five thousand decided on Australia or New Zealand. Joseph was among the many from Staffordshire.

Already toiling in the coalmines aged nine and illiterate, the 1870 Elementary Education Act reeled him back to school until he was twelve. Straightaway his dad restored him to the pit known locally as the "Hell Hole" with its long steep gradients, heat and grotty state of affairs.

Life changed for Joseph when his dad was killed. And little guessing it was in a pit accident. He had been a 'butty miner' – one who controlled recruitment into his team. The role made him and his family better off than the average Silverdale hewer in a village that was growing. By 1881 it had just shy of six thousand inhabitants. Up three and three quarter thousand from 1841. Such was the draw of coal and ironstone.

However, 1883 and 1884 saw strikes and a depression in the industry causing Joseph to plump for a radical change of climate. He took with him the brownie points of having become Silverdale's chief orator.

Lay preaching was his bedrock before trade unionism tickled his fancy. Before reaching his quarter century in age he had been elected successively to all the executive positions in his union lodge. Political issues interested, resulting in him supporting tariff protection as a method of improving his industry's working conditions. It was the perfect fodder for life in the Antipodes that saw him rise to be Australia's Prime Minister in 1913. Within five years he got dubbed his knighthood.

During a six-year spell as Australian High Commissioner in London Joseph made a brief return to Silverdale for old times' sake, and was given the freedom of Newcastle-under-Lyme. The honour though wouldn't keep him in his old neck of the woods. He passed away in Sydney in 1947. The famed Australian sculptor Wallace Anderson made a bronze bust that shows off Joseph's distinguished beard and whiskers. It's on Prime Ministers Avenue in Ballarat's exotic Botanical Gardens, and a target for sulphur-crested cockatoos. The smart, gold rush town in Victoria is a far cry from the 'Hell Hole'.

Damning and blasting that I forgot to cross-examine Ejaz about strawberry yoghurt chicken and still penitent over the parrot incident, I drove the Newcastle-under-Lyme bypass alone. I promised myself to later investigate how much the town has changed. Or maybe not.

Yes, yes, a veil had been drawn over the desultory little petting zoo of cages on stilts in the strip of park opposite the Borough Arms Hotel. The alopecia blighted chinchilla – or was it a guinea pig? – and the mangy lop-eared bunnies were pitiful, even at a glance. Instead there were rumours of chuggers – those infuriatingly chirpy charity muggers – being a public pain. And, I'd earwigged that Syd's Bar – once disastrously owned by Alan Hudson the former Stoke City midfielder – had become another curry house toting balti, bhuna and pathia, and made me think of Fred.

Alan, who ended up hitting rock bottom living in a homeless hostel, had banned anybody wearing a leather jacket from the pub, which meant the majority of the clientele. This was after Andy, a South African I knew, the last survivor of an army unit fighting in the Angolan Bush War, laid out six bikers with a beer tray over a trivial mumble about Kaffir lime leaves.

Aside to this, local councillors were in a lather of excitement. The brown-field corridor between Stoke and Newcastle now had a proper name: Ceramic Valley. Plug the past and investment from the world over will definitely, definitely, definitely create a zone of utopian enterprise. Anyway that's the hope, and the city of Stoke-on-Trent is home to bet365. I left well alone.

The outbound from Newcastle Knutton Lane was clarted. Anyhow, no worry. In the tortoise-slow traffic I noticed stuff. The fire station had benefitted from a facelift. And a burnt-out car wallowing in a wide puddle suggested a recent fire practice. Further practice and the car might have escaped with only scorch marks.

Across the road at the Gordon Banks Sports Centre freestyle footballers were showing-off, and basketballs were doubtless being slam-dunked somewhere inside. The long retired goalie had enthused how proud and honoured he was having the Centre named after him when it opened in 2010. "It's like winning the World Cup again," he said.

Lord love a duck! How doubly proud he must be having his bronze likeness, goalie gloves in one hand, lifting the Jules Rimet World Cup trophy, stood smack bang in front of the Britannia Stadium on Gordon Banks Way. The statue is the work of figurative sculptor Andy Edwards.

The same Andy who created the Beatles statues at Liverpool's Pierhead. And who, over a year, collaborated with sculptors Julian Jeffrey and Carl Payne to forge the three-pose, life size and a half, Sir Stanley Matthews sculpture.

Braving the elements the dramatic art piece is aligned towards the club's old Victoria Ground where the star did his wizard dribbling. Everything is historically correct – right down to the last eyelet of his football boots. All the balls are the right era. The strip too. Even the rope holding up Sir Stan's shorts, so as not to embarrass himself upon making his Stoke debut as a whippersnapper.

Turning into Arthur Street I saw my old house. Uniform red brick and semi-detached, it was still there behind the privet hedge.

Craning my neck, I could see down the alley to cane-climbing runner beans and sweet peas. I remembered the back garden as brown earth brightened by groundsel and sparse dandelions. Some of which I picked and put in a jam jar – Sunday lunch decoration for the kitchen table. A table laid specially for my girlfriend 'Shotgun'. Honestly, it was a term of endearment. It really was. Except to her face.

Barging in on her father being nasty to her mother she threateningly lisped to blast him through a wall. Given the family home was a castle she would have needed at least both barrels. The anecdote made me try extra hard.

Regretfully the splattered coalbunker dissuaded fireside cosiness. Being blanket-wrapped from cold is never a good look. And sinews of scraggy roast stuck between her teeth made her irritable. As did Jethro Tull's 'Locomotive Breath'.

I suggested a stroll to Rotterdam. Shotgun appeared at first keen then became quizzical as I pointed to a crescent of nondescript housing across scrub ground where hawthorn trees made a pretty poor fist at growing and grass couldn't quite be bothered to look green. "Never had a clue why it's called Rotterdam," I said, "but from there we can get to a ginormous slag heap. It's worth seeing." She seemed to scowl reluctance and when underway thought the saggy teats on a vagrant mutt more interesting.

"Find the puppies and I might give you a kiss," she blackmailed.

I gave a sweep of the coal black shadows along the Lyme Brook. Nothing. Just broken glass and rusted cans, eddying sweet wrappers, snagged pearls of cellophane on bramble, and plastic bags wrapped around roots. A leather boot nurtured snails and woodlice.

"Hey, look at this," I said, hoping the boot would do. A mocking magpie gave Shotgun's answer. Love wasn't to be.

Alan, I learned, had been dead a decade or more. "Black lung," said the corner shop lady, her hair a net of curlers. "Happened before the old colliery became the Void."

The Void. Total dereliction. I slouched off to see what had occurred to Alan's nemesis. The final shift of miners went down into North Staffordshire's last deep coal mine at 6am on Christmas Eve, 1998.

I found Silverdale Country Park and heard a skylark. A chap jabbed happily at squidgy ground with a garden spade. In a wheelbarrow lay sapling willows. Perfect for a home somewhere around the large pond, which had to be the Furnace Pool I had heard of. Armed with a question I advanced to distract the jabber.

Trev was a volunteer. "We don't call this the Void anymore ... well, we do. But in nice way," he said. He explained the park had two distinct areas. Tongue-in-cheek they were called the Void, which was the watery bit, and the Waste Farm, which I clearly saw was the hilly bit. "It was rubbish here for about ten years but now, wow!" Trev enthused. "Hard to believe this used to be a pit."

'Yeah," I agreed, looking at the hilly bit.

The colliery spoil remains stockpiled and it's obvious where. Plateaux of different heights are akin to Table Mountain lookalikes of Lilliputian scale. Each have steep embankments which natural grass and young trees colonise. "You get great views from the highest point," said Trev. I took his word for it and mentioned the skylark. That set him off. He spoke of bees and orchids, lapwings and herons, hunting buzzards and visiting osprey. A rare Butcher Bird, too.

"And the skylark?" I reminded.

"Oh, there're loads of them."

"Any four-legged animals? Fox? Hare?"

"All of them and more."

I mused upon what lay beneath my feet. "Bet badgers think they've found the great halls of Emperor Brock."

The pièce de résistance happened in January 2015. The park's watery part was designated as a Site of Biological Importance. A success, Trev said, down to community spirit. The comment prompted me to ask how the community coped after the mine's closure. "Badly," was Trev's reply.

He was "on the railways" and witnessed 60 078 'Slioch' on its curving decent of the 'Madeley Chord' line. The heavy diesel locomotive was performing the last rites of rail-borne Silverdale coal. In tow were the many rail trucks heaped with the final stockpiles. Trev remembered feeling "sick in the gut". Planting trees was cathartic.

"What about the miners' emotions," I pumped.

His look was sorrowful. "If you can't guess that, try asking in 'The Vine'. They serve cheap beer when Stoke City's on the telly. But they aren't today."

So, another pub lunch. A normal priced pint of Bass and a packet of cheese and onion crisps suited me fine. In Silverdale High Street 'The Vine', ticked out with red window frames, welcomed, although I chanced on quiet. A log fire smoked. A strategic ceiling fan dispelled the worst of it. The dartboard and juke box were predictable. Patches of flowery carpet matching the floor were stuck to the bar sides ensuring the knees of the barstool perching were comfortable. "You lost or sussing the joint out for Jason Dale?"

Having shaken my noggin as answer to both questions the inquisitive and burly, stubble-chinned twenty-something lad, introduced himself as Lorry. A painter and decorator, his glass looked half empty.

A wall poster crowed that Jason Dale was 'the ultimate Elvis tribute act' and 'direct from his US tour'. "He's a Stokie," said Lorry. "Everyone knows him. He's been the living King for years. As a young mite he got on the bloody ballroom stage with Freddie Star at Trentham Gardens."

"What, for a bit of monkeying around?"

"Eh?"

"Trentham's monkeys. The hundred and forty brown-haired Barbary macaques that sit and yawn among the bluebells."

"Oh yeah, yeah. I hear yer." Lorry chuckled. "Some of Freddie's antics wouldn't go amiss in the Monkey Forest.

"Anyway, they did 'Blue Suede Shoes'. Now Jason's got the sideburns. But here he'll have a job matching Whoops Celtic Apocalypse."

Although tempted, I chose not to ask. Instead, I heard about camaraderie and its fate.

"A paint brush and roller doesn't get you seeing a lot of mates every day," Lorry confided. "My dad had it different. He's unemployed now but before that he was down the pits. Every older bloke around here was. Yeah, there were accidents. Lost toes. Lost fingers, like the landlord here. But everybody just got on with it. Enjoyed the social life. Nowadays the face workers are security guards or hospital porters. Some work for the council. A mate's dad works in a quarry. Machine-fitters got jobs okay.

"Apart from footie community spirit's gone tits-up. People don't watch each other's backs like they used to. But dad says that started in the eighties with Maggie Thatcher. The pit closure strikes split pit families down the middle. The strikes went on so long some went back to work to support their families. My uncle did. He had four small kids. Dad stuck to it."

I remembered how it was.

"And Dad hasn't spoken to my uncle since. Course, it's affected me. I take my frustration out off-roading in Haying Wood. It's a 'Landy' zone – Land Rovers. Slippery hills, engine roar, and loads of mud. Love it. Though probably pisses off the wildlife." Lorry finished his pint.

I bought him a refill before leaving. Doing so I wondered if Trev knew from where the furred and feathered population might have come that crowds the Void. I had second thoughts. The notion probably wouldn't have curried favour.

LESSON FOURTEEN

Paws and Pigman

*"If you hold a cat by the tail you learn
things you cannot learn any other way."*
Mark Twain, American humorist.

Hobbit-sized Milami an obvious no-no, Kolya, a testosterone-engine Skoda, had made it a pleasant enough family tour until the previous day's show of dissent.

My convoluted suggestion was we stop off at Brewood church to see a stained glass version of an intact St Chad, Staffordshire's patron saint. He held a depiction of Lichfield Cathedral, a reminder of where his actual head was stashed before it was nicked during the Reformation. Mona, mum of Ali my wife, wrinkled her nose, the signal for 'not bloody likely'. Now keeping the same nose as far away from the breakfast fish as practicable without having to appear rude, she bit into a raw onion slice.

Rain spattering the windows I announced the new itinerary: vomiting lion, a bit of exercise, and pot luck with monster adventures. Ali's translation wasn't forthcoming and the nose didn't move.

Wiping his mouth with a napkin, saucy smoked haddock and Parmesan omelette devoured, Romi raised a digit. "Vhy is Veston oonder a lizard?" My father-in-law's hobbled English had reason. With a laugh, Ali will describe herself as "European mongrel".

In any language Romi's was a fair question. I shrugged. After all, the four of us had spent the night eccentrically accommodated in Weston-under-Lizard. At Weston Park, in matter of fact. Half the summer V Festival music is performed here to thousands of sweaty, scantily clad arm-waving youths.

Pixie Lott, Passion Pit, and Frightened Rabbit. That's the sort of stuff. A weekend event with the other half in Essex, acts swap venue Saturday and Sunday.

"The Lizard is the name of the hill over there in Shrophire. S'pose lizards lived on it." I held up by palms. Helpless.

Romi seemed to accept my answer when, just audible, came distant salvos of gunfire. "I think zay are shooting de lizards."

"Can't be. Must be shooting pheasants."

"Zo, zay got aw de lizards?"

Breakfast had been my attempt at making omelette Arnold Bennett for three.

Something auspicious definitely felt in order. The chefs at the Savoy created the concoction for the Potteries' writer, so delighting him he insisted on it being made wherever he travelled. Us having bedded down in the Temple of Diana seemed deserving.

Domed and built in the 1760s the temple has an awful lot of light – plenty to spy the littlest fish bone. And, as temples go, it quite shakes the times – Wi-Fi and a mechanical dishwasher were wholly unexpected. Central heating kept the marrow warm from the chill mists creeping across a thousand acres of 'Capability' Brown parkland. Ali and Mona, her mum, were grateful.

The Temple – an orangery actually – is a gem of James Paine's. The eighteenth-century architect, the same chap who designed Chatsworth House, called it "my greenhouse at Weston". The clothes yanked from the washing machine reassured that none of us appeared to have grown in the night.

By mid morning we crammed aboard Kolya. Romi had luggage and Pac A Macs ingeniously stowed. And oh goody, the rain turned from drizzle to deluge. The lion would doubtlessly impress.

Pretty sharpish Blymhill church tower looked venerable amid ancient trees. A sodden field of stubble nuzzled against the perfectly trimmed but drippy churchyard privet hedge. Rural divineness. And, as a bonus, St Mary's brags the odd. In the south aisle roof are rarities: dormer windows installed in 1836 because the church was so dark inside. But these are not the reason why I brought the parents-in-law. Getting soggier by the second I attracted their gaze up to the running gutters.

A gargoyle. Two paws braced on the wall, two on the buttress, its open maw, tongue green with moss, spewed into a downpipe.

Affectionately called the 'vomiting-lion', it's quite an attraction.

In old Greek, both 'vomiting' and 'preaching' are translatable using the same word. One has to ponder whether a sculptor suffering sermonising windbags got his own back. That really would be classical.

The lion's been admired by Sir Simon Jenkins – the journalist, broadcaster, and writer who doesn't often use his title. The *Independent* wrote of him being "so grand he really should be bought and preserved by the National Trust, so that successive generations can admire the wondrous architecture and exquisite furniture of his mind." Simon became the Trust's Chairman, instead. He loves anything that is old and beautiful.

By a warm fireside and cuddling a whisky I had the good fortune to mention Blymhill to him. "I included it in my book," he said. There you have it. St Mary's is one *England's Thousand Best Churches.*

Mona, too, liked the lion. Though the performance wasn't worth her getting saturated, she remonstrated. As if in apology the leaden skies began to pale. I gladdened at my forward planning of buying 'Bay Chum Spiders'.

"It's cheering up," I said, crossing my fingers. Oh, the scowl. Best omit showing off a very old milestone under a hazelnut tree on the A41's grass verge, I decided. Anyway, the interesting surveyor's benchmark used as a reference point in altitude measurement had eroded.

Beside the expanse of rough grass, dandelion clocks, and daisies that is Milford Common I parked by the start of the Heart of England Way – a 105 mile trek ending at Bourton on the Water in the Cotswolds. Something for the bucket list. But not today, thank you. Facing the common gapes the National Trust's Shugborough estate entrance. Go through to the county's official museum. It wasn't for us, either.

I rallied my troops. Cannock Chase began a short stroll away and it was full of beasties – even werewolves. Ali translated. Romi's face lit up. He was game.

Mona's scowl, slowly, slowly in abeyance, returned forcefully. She wagged a finger. A warning. The sky stayed cloud-hulked.

A gentle uphill and we were in the woods. "Nothing to be afraid of. We've got hours of daylight." I considered the possibility that I was reassuring myself.

Walkers somehow keep stumbling on meat-stripped deer carcasses.

The culprits? Big cats, some say. There is another explanation. Over twenty 'official' sightings of werewolves have been reported on Cannock Chase … amongst other horrors.

Whoop and howl, seeing the Pig-Man was more rare.

He began as 1940s gossip. Half-human and half-swine, he was allegedly spied by idiots straying into Cannock Chase woods after dark. Witnesses spoke of a mortal in tattered clothes having a distorted face, a palpable snout, and a shrill squeal.

The story goes after the Second World War British and American military scientists joined forces to conduct a series of iffy eugenics experiments. Those tests went too far. In the hope of obtaining a creature worth testing, a woman was abducted. She was impregnated with an artificially created human-pig DNA seed.

Boffins monitored her for ten months. Nothing. Then, all of a sudden, gosh. A baby with an outsized head and a big snout, like a pig's, was born. This strangeness later escaped and hid in the woods. The leafy woods, silent of squeals and howls, we now trod, full of hiding places and paths. Numerous paths.

Mona picked up and inspected an acorn. "Gebissen," she observed, 'bitten', distracting my eeny meeny miny mo method of path selection.

"We can't ignore Bigfoot," I said. Ali gave my arm a right jab. "Obviously that's people messing about with Chewbacca on Photoshop," I riposted, hurriedly.

Still. On the 21 of January 1879, a labourer was employed to take a cart of luggage from Ranton to Woodcock, which is beyond Shropshire's Newport. Coming back, his horse knackered, it had gone ten o'clock when he reached the bridge over the Birmingham and Liverpool Canal.

A "strange black creature with great white eyes" sprang from the roadside plantation and sat astride the horse. Brave, the bloke tried to shove the thing off with his whip. Horror of horrors the whip went through it. A day or so later a policeman made a home visit. He bore news of the apparition that gave the labourer the yips.

"That, sir, was the Man-Monkey," the constable said.

A sighting on the Cannock to Rugeley road sparked contemporary alerts. It has to be Bigfoot, folk bleated in February 1995. A lady called Jackie Haughton had to swerve her car to narrowly avoid an RTA with something large and shambling. A fleeting encounter but enough for a description: "man-like and tall, very hairy, with two self-illuminating, glowing red eyes."

Three years on, similar happened to another motorist who managed a lengthier recount: "A tall, man-like figure, around 6-feet 8 inches, very strong-looking and with a darkish, blacky-brown coat. Sort of crouching forward, it turned and looked straight at us. I still get goosebumps."

Spring 2004, and the Iron Age hill-fort Castle Ring brought a further turn up. A 7-foot creature was described as having short, shiny, dark brown hair, large head. Its eyes, too, glowed bright red.

Bigfoot was getting taller. The greenhouse effect?

Then came autumn 2008's wee incident. A "terrifying beast" chased a carload of locals in the small hours.

"This thing was the shape of a human," one swore, "but stood about 7 to 8-foot tall. As soon as it realised we had seen it, it stood up straight and ran towards us. This thing was definitely not human. It was huge! It wasn't just tall, but broad and stocky, too. I don't know whether it was flying or jumping or what."

And before I forget, the-thingumy-whatzit made an "owl-like cry".

At face value it knocked the theory of Derek Crawley, chairman of the Staffordshire Mammal Group, on the head. He suggested Bigfoot or the Man-Monkey could actually be a panther in a tree whose branches got mistaken for arms. What a scream, a barn owl might add.

"Cannock Chase is a hot spot for panther sightings. Tell Romi and Mona that." I said to Ali.

"Panther?" Romi had seized on the word. Dead leaves rustled. "PANTHER?" said Mona suddenly startled. A grey fluffy tail shot up a tree.

It was Ali's turn to show the admonishing finger. "Oh very well done. You've actually got them nervous."

And I hadn't even mentioned the uber-snake, a possible fourteen-footer headlining the *Birmingham Post*. Powerful head. Colouring that contrasted beautifully against the bracken fern.

"Ali," I whispered, "remember the bloke at Slitting Mill pool who was swigging a drink when something very long moved on the bank? 'It sort of wriggled. The whole body seemed to sort of shake and wobble'. I think those were his words."

Ali was rational as ever. "'Swigging a drink' are the operative ones. As enchanting as these woods are, shall we go find your special bridge before seeing anything bigger than a squirrel?"

Behind us we heard barking. I had to chuckle. "So no tales of the phantom black dog?"

"No."

But nothing to stop me later telling the story of Freda the Great Dane, I thought

A path hugged the Shugborough Estate boundary fence. We followed it and arrived at the Estate entrance at Great Haywood. Fairly sure of the way, I led us through and along the drive until, almost at the railway bridge, I stopped to point at a grass hill topped by a stone arch. "It's the Triumphal Arch, a copy of Hadrian's Gate in Athens," I explained. "A stand out Georgian beauty."

Built in 1765, it commemorates Admiral Anson. Shugborough Hall is the former home of the Anson family, the Earls of Lichfield. The admiral circumnavigated the globe and oversaw the Royal Navy during the Seven Years' War. His likeness and that of his wife sit as busts in a bit of upper stonework above the actual arch. Peter Scheemakers, the illustrious Flemish sculptor, carved them. Maybe he's better known for having chiselled the Shakespeare memorial in Westminster Abbey's Poets' Corner.

Mona thought the hill better suited to sheep.

Tucked away in some Shugborough evergreens is another of Scheemakers works. The rustic looking Shepherd's Monument is a lot smaller than the Triumphal Arch. Within it the Scheemakers relief carving show a woman and three shepherds, two of which point to a tomb. Below someone unknown carved eight riddling letters: O U O S V A V V. They are 'bookended' by the letters 'D M' – standing for Dis Manibus or 'dedicated to the shades'. What bafflement for cryptanalysts. Suggestions for the meaning of the letters range from the showing the location of the Holy Grail to a secret love story. The code had defied Bletchley Park codebreakers, not to mention the efforts of Josiah Wedgwood, Charles Darwin, and Charles Dickens. A National Trust spokesman has managed a straight face saying: "We get five or six people a week who believe they have solved the code so we are a bit wary of them now."

As for the Hall its façade too boggles the mind, purely because it's so huge. Both Romi and Mona seeming impressed we bore right on a gravel path and down to the longest packhorse bridge in England – fourteen span arches across the River Trent. Once, there had been forty.

"The Essex Bridge," I said.

Romi became questioning. "It goes to ver zay have ze uzza half of ze Vee music festival?"

Ali tutored the general geography.

I added that the Trent's junction with the River Sow lies 100 yards upstream along banks abundant with purple Himalayan balsam and rosebay willow herb, white elderflower and Queen Anne's lace; then I did the history bit.

The Earl of Essex, who like many nobles didn't stay put in their county of name, had the bridge painstakingly thrown over the river in 1550. Just so Queen Elizabeth I could trot across for a bit of carefree woodland hunting knowing her rival Mary Queen of Scots was safely immured in Tutbury. Characterful and pointed, niches at intervals along the bridge's sides gave foot-sloggers room to avoid trotting steeds or to hold their noses at a trundling manure cart.

The bridge also helped inspire the fantasies of J.R.R. Tolkein. In *The Tale of the Sun And The Moon* – part of the *The Book of Lost Tales* – the village of Tavrobel is breathed life. It's based, says Christopher Tolkien, J.R.R.'s son and literary executor, on Great Haywood.

The evidence is compelling. Tavrobel has a bridge where two rivers – the Gruir and the Afros – meet. Has to be the Trent and Sow. In the tale, Eriol is urged to take up the hospitality of a gnome called Gilfanon "whose ancient house – the house of a hundred chimneys, stands nigh the bridge of Tavrobel".

Shugborough has eighty chimneys. Picture fires lit in all the draughty rooms on a murky winter's afternoon, the light turning dimpsey. Doubtless the sight, seen from the footpath we walked along, warranted 'House of a Hundred Chimneys'. That it enraptured a traumatised soldier fascinated by myth and mystery is very likely.

Tolkien had seen action in the Somme in France. Returning to Blighty in need of rehab he was stationed on Cannock Chase in the winter of 1916-1917. Recently wed, he and his wife Edith lived in a Great Haywood cottage. Tavrobel seeded in his mind.

And J.R.R. and Edith were forced to be neighbourly. Always an important place for the modern military half-a-million soldiers bided on the Chase during World War One.

Poignantly, a short pootle away down a couple of lanes from Great Haywood something extraordinary is buried under Brocton tree roots and undergrowth – a model of the Messines terrain. It covers a hundred and thirty square feet.

The model depicts the Belgian town – the place Adolf Hitler was shot in the arm and awarded the Iron Cross – as captured by New Zealand troops in June 1917.

Troops that returned to England did so with an adopted black and white spotted Harlequin Great Dane called Freda. Amidst the death and destruction she had brought Kiwi soldiers warmth and solace.

And it was these men that supervised German prisoners of war to painstakingly recreate Messines both as a training aid for odds-on cannon fodder heading to Passchendaele and a lasting tribute to fallen colleagues on a battlefield that left fifty thousand gone to glory.

Perfect in every way are the shelled and crumbling streets, shops, homes and churches in the aftermath of the Battle of Messines Ridge. Every nook and cranny is exact. Every cobble. Every bombed building from basement to rooftop. Every trench. Every hedgerow contour.

Precipitated by the detonation of nineteen enormous mines under the German front lines – made famous in the Aussie feature film *Beneath Hill 60* – Messines Ridge was the first time Australians and New Zealanders had fought side by side since the Gallipoli campaign of 1915. And Aussie and Kiwi would argue over the laurels for the victory at Messines.

Soberly, Cannock Chase holds many, many war dead. Four thousand eight hundred and fifty-five lie in the German Cemetery. Casualties from both world wars.

At Brocton, on the edge of bracken, bramble, and gorse is a solitary grave. The headstone reads:

'FREDA – MASCOT NEW ZEALAND RIFLES 1918
FRIENDS OF CANNOCK CHASE'.

On top of the headstone are pebbles arranged with purpose unknown by persons unknown. On Anzac Day 2013 a uniformed New Zealand representative placed a Dolores Cross – simple and hand-made of weaved Harakeke – on the grave. Harakeke is flax native to New Zealand and is chosen because it grows plentifully and creates an intimate link between the homeland and those New Zealanders who went to fight in both World Wars and never returned.

Why Dolores Cross? Well, 'Dolores' is Latin for 'sorrows', and relates to the Virgin Mary. She is 'Maria de los Dolores' – 'Our Lady of Sorrows' or 'Mary of Sorrows'. As such, the name 'Dolores Cross' for memorial purpose means "the cross of sorrows".

Freda's collar is kept at the Army Museum at Waiouru.

As for the Essex Bridge that's simply seen as a short cut across the river. For us, it was perfect for competitive Poohsticks.

"Tomorrow, Romi," I said, "I shall photograph you by the statues of Sir Stanley Matthews."

Romi gave me the thumbs up. "The Vizard of de Dribble," he said. "Zen ve zee de Vedgvud Portland Vase?"

"Yep, we will indeed," I assured. Four years it had taken Josiah Wedgwood to get his famous blue-black jasper pot with two handles right. Trial and error until beauty emerged at the 25th attempt. Son Josiah II had helped, fiddling and faddling with the pot's white cameo figures. On one side the mythological marriage of the Greek sea-gods Peleus and Thetis. On the reverse Ariadne of labyrinth and Minotaur fame languishing on Naxos. The inspiration had been the first century BC Barberini Vase, one of the finest examples of ancient cameo glass in the world.

During 1845's winter a fat vandal with a booze problem waltzed into the British Museum and smashed the ancient gem into two hundred shards. Wedgwood's replica enabled the artefact to be painstakingly and faithfully pieced back together. Lucky stuff. Today producing a Portland Vase remains perhaps the ultimate challenge of a Wedgwood potter's skills and artistry.

On the first occasion I saw Josiah's masterpiece displayed at Barlaston's 'World of Wedgwood' the Stokie accented audio commentary had the strange effect of stinging my eyes with tears.

Then again the story of Major Cecil Wedgwood had me fight back an actual urge to blub. At the outbreak of the Word War One Cecil, federated Stoke-on-Trent's first mayor, was head of the family firm. Aged fifty-three he was too old to enlist. Doing so anyway and bushy moustache trimmed he raised two battalions, the 7th and 8th North Staffords, recruiting mainly potters. His collected letters describe life in the trenches. The care he took to secure his men clean billets earned them the moniker 'Major Wedgwood's pets'. On the third day of the Battle of the Somme in July 1916, Cecil copped it along with many 'pets'.

Letters written to his wife Lucie gave eyewitness accounts of his last moments. Shot in the neck by a sniper, Cecil was urging on his beloved men with a battle cry of "Come on, North Staffords!" Such waste of talent.

In Barlaston's demonstration area Mary, petite and thin paintbrush in hand and was three quarters of an hour into deftly painting a bone china plate. "Been doing this thirty years, duck," she smiled, answering my question. "So I must love it here. If you cut me in half I'll have 'Wedgwood' running all the way down through me, like a stick of rock."

A flight of rain-slippery steps led down to the Trent and Mersey Canal. The puddled towpath went in the direction of the car. By nightfall we were in Madeley, a doable stomp from Keele University. Ali, full of common sense, had booked us into a pub having Pedigree on tap.

Not wanting to put Mona off, neither Ali nor I mentioned the village pond becoming a fish carpet of roach, perch, carp, bream, and tench. Five thousand fish snuffed it. Agricultural silage, apparently. Dads and mums had scrambled to aid the floundering survivors. Paddling pools and a baby bath became makeshift fishponds. Children armed with buckets and tiddler nets pulled their weight. Firefighters ran hoses, oxygenating the water. Herculean efforts saved hundreds.

"It had been quite a battle," the barmaid said, and laughed when a lad pressed the digital jukebox for 'Monster Mash'. Serendipity. I imagined odd creatures of Cannock Chase twisting along.

Reflecting on the day Ali and Romi agreed with one another. Sometimes I do things that makes the brain hurt.

LESSON FIFTEEN

Cheese and Chariot

"Life. A spiritual pickle preserving the body from decay."
Ambrose Bierce, American Writer,
journalist and editor.

On a grey Cologne afternoon, the brightest light came from the TV in the corner of my parents-in-law's sitting room. The travel programme bored. The presenter, an uber-healthy woman prattled on about "Englisch Essen und berühmte Leute" – English food and famous people. Her discourse rambled onto oranges and Sir Richard Arkwright. And, whilst I wracked my brain to link the two, the shot panned from open countryside, across a lovely cricket pitch, a landscaped garden, to the orangery of a stately mansion.

"Seine ... ist es Dunstall Halle!" I declared, pointing. Knock me sideways, it really was Dunstall Hall.

Romi asked if he'd been there. I said no, we'd missed it on our diverting tour. How was it I was so lax?

Arkwright, one of the eighteenth-century's self-made men, was taught to read and write by his cousin. Inventing the Spinning Jenny – a frame that made it easy to spin thread from wool or yarn – and opening the world's first water-powered cotton mill in 1771 coined him an engineering pioneer. Huge wealth accumulated. His son, Richard junior, spent a portion of it buying Dunstall Hall as a present for his own lad, Charles.

What isn't common knowledge, the fellow who sold the Hall to junior was John Meek. My great-great-grandad Commander Edmund Peel RN married his daughter Lucy in stout-towered and crenelated Barton-under-Needwood church. The curate who pronounced them man and wife was

Thomas Gisborne a member of the Clapham Sect. With William Wilberforce as its centre of gravity the group fought for the abolition of the slave trade in England.

Thomas' assistance meanwhile had ensured Edmund abundant topping for his ship's biscuits.

Instead of wittering on about bloody oranges the German TV presenter should have chatted about cheese. She really should. John Meek's fortune lay in selling cakes and truckles of the stuff. Cheese firm and elastic or soft and gooey. Cheese mellow and buttery or dense and crumbly. Yes, yes, cheese boasts nil vitamin C. But, wonderfulness upon wonderfulness, consider the calcium. And phenylethylamine. Now that's an aphrodisiac. Aided by humble cheese on crackers, Edmund and Lucy brought nine children into the world. That would not happen with oranges.

Amongst the local Shropshire blue, the Derby, and the Cheshire, say hurrah for the scrumptious Staffordshire, a clothbound cheese, whose unique flavour and texture has its origins with Leek's Cistercian monks. They invented the recipe seven hundred years ago or more. Today, the Staffordshire Cheese Company makes it in the town. The taste comes from their dairy cows' top secret diet. Which I guess must include Staffordshire grass.

I jogged Romi's memory of his first nibble and he gave a beatific smile, which until that moment had been reserved for the Craster kipper.

Unfortunately when John Meek hopped the twig the family's cheese connection, in the business sense, had 'gone for a Burton'. I clarified with Romi this meant 'vanished without trace'. It had nothing to do with actor Richard or film director Tim. Burton, I said, is a town on which Germany indirectly made a huge impact. A town very near Dunstall Hall.

The informal, very British, slang expression 'gone for a Burton' first appeared in print in the *New Statesman* on 30 August 1941, a gloss over for 'crash'. In the *Aeronautical Review* of March 1942, it definitely meant 'killed in action'.

The first 'spoken' use came in *Australian Women's Weekly* magazine in an article about the Hollywood actor John Justin, a Brit. An RAF pilot, he was briefly released from duty to work on a propaganda film *The Gentle Sex*, designed to improve the image of the women's Auxiliary Territorial Service – the ATS.

My mum was ATS and proud of her sergeant stripes. When not double declutching her 'Yellow Peril' sport car at speed her voice barked PT instructions at the firm-breasted in plimsolls. Which image needed improving?

Justin, a fledgling pedagogue to be frank, didn't answer that. Instead, he relived a lucky escape:

"In July 1940 I had just been made a flying instructor when I hit a tree, pranged my crate, and smashed myself up. I nearly died after that shaky do,

… I was lucky, for I thought I'd 'gone for a Burton'."

There it was: the black humour of pilots hooked on beer. Off finding a pint of the best – a Burton – explained any absence however permanent. It was the way of coping with a mate missing in action or to a lesser extent the demise of a small camping tent after a hornet liked my shaving cream.

Brewers, though, accepted anybody's custom. Beer demand peaked in Britain in the 1880s. Although in steady decline elsewhere ever since, Burton-on-Trent has bucked the trend, and continues to produce beer in lashings.

Local brewers – Bass, Truman's, and Marston's – plied their delights under the umbrella Burton Ales. Former Bass managing director Bob Ricketts mused: "It was not a question of the breweries being in the town centre, it was the town centre that was in the middle of the breweries." Burton today brews more beer than ever before, around fifteen per cent of the UK's total output.

There has to be a secret, and there is: The 'Burton snatch'. This I can assure is nothing vulgar but to do with the water.

My flat-capped friend Anthony describes himself as a 'bevvying Burtoner' and he explained all. Not though before the terrifying incident of the 'Farm-foods chariot'.

Anthony and Marmy, his pongy longhaired dachshund, either end of an extending leash, had pulled up beside the curved iron Andresey footbridge – the one with the embossed white flowers. It crosses Peel's Cut, once taking River Trent water to a Robert Peel cotton mill. As a norm the Cut is peaceful. Swans love it. Willows are lazily floppy. In spring daffodils bow and bob in the wind. Should it blow in the right direction, you can smell the Marmite factory.

Inside, Marmite's secret ingredient is kept in a sealed grey box. The factory is so computerised and automated just fifty-nine employees are required to oversee production of two hundred and fifty brown jars a minute. That's twenty-five million a year. Made of pharmaceutical quality glass from Düsseldorf's Gerresheimer works, they do a linear jiggle down to the labelling machine.

The simmering 'marmite' stew-pot logo dates from the 1920s, a constant on the label that on occasion has had the odd tweak – the special edition Ma'amite label for the Diamond Jubilee or the limited run of heart-shaped labels on Champagne Marmite for 2008's Valentine's Day. There might be samples still hiding in kitchens. High salt content – flavour essential – and low water content – texturally essential – aid preservation. Bacteria finding it hard to grow, notionally Marmite lasts forever. Fine idea, then, that a laser burns a 'best before date' traceable to within a minute of production.

Remember, Marmite only exists because of beer. A German chemist, Justus Von Liebig, had recognised the value of yeast as a brewery waste product in the 1800s. News from Europe was worth picking up.

Mr F. V. A. Smith, call sign XSR, tapped into the epoch-making. A Burton radio ham, he got his first licence in July 1914. One month later he intercepted a London-bound message from the Marconi spark transmitter at Poldhu in Cornwall. The message survives in Burton upon Trent Amateur Radio Club archives. Announcing the mobilisation of Russian, French and Belgian troops it was outbreak eve of the First World War.

Marmite came into own. It protected British troops from the evils of beriberi.

I vouch for its value too. The rumour that Marmite wards off midges is true. After chomping a Marmite smeared pitta bread an Aswan felucca excursion on the Nile left me unbitten. Impressive, I thought. The friend I was with loathed Marmite passionately. Egypt's midges thought her scrummy.

The Marmite Food Extract Company began tickling the love or hate taste buds on a bucket-sized scale from disused malt houses in Burton's Cross Street. Nowadays large tankers collect the brewery waste. Molson Coors is sited bang next door and Marston's and Bass are just down the road. The waste doesn't have to go far. First and foremost hop remains are sieved out to leave citrus smelling slurry sold to farmers as soil conditioner. Converted to flammable gas fluid effluent heats the factory's boilers.

The Burton factory is home to both veggie Marmite and beefy Bovril. Combined, six thousand tonnes are produced annually. Eighty per cent of which is Marmite. The percentage proved decisive. For what it's worth, Bovrilina instead of Marmy really wouldn't have suited Anthony's doglet.

She sat resigned by the footbridge where, set in the wall, is the grey head stone from the old town hall. On it two beasts hold a shield and are badly weathered. Obvious really, suffering the elements since the 1770s. The stone had deflected Anthony and my attentions. Marmy wuffed her warning too late.

As a general rule a shopping trolley is transport from till to car. And I've heard a Farmfoods trolley is usually brim-full of frozen discounted fare. Aimed at us came a branded whoosh-rattle express holding a frosty-eyed yowling urchin tot. Panicked, Marmy leapt sideways and made a splash, leash unwinding like a sprung tape measure. Propelled by what I took to be scruffy parents – the mum videoing thrills on a smart phone – the trolley crossed the line. Us boring obstructions merited receding obscenities.

I gawped in their wake. Some people deserve a summons. Yet I imagined denizens of Burton's huge peripheral council estates were blasé of such receipt.

Faith must therefore be placed in Darwin's theory of natural selection.

The Cut was confusion. Wings beat angrily. Swan on the attack, a floundering Marmy focused on doggy-paddle. Quickly stomach flat Anthony thrashed his flat cap single-handedly at the incensed bird, the other hand reached to grab Marmy's collar.

This wasn't the Burton Snatch, either.

"Hold my pissing ankles!" Anthony spat. Burtoners are little different to other Staffies: hardy, stubborn, independent-minded people, short-fused in the face of ineptitude. Know that, and you won't take offence.

Slithering into reverse Anthony dragged Marmy's bedraggled form up the bank to safety. The swan glared down its beak with loathing. My friend rubbed his arm. Although bruised he would live. "May Her Majesty gorge on Burton swan," he grimaced.

Only later, over a second pint of medicinal Marston's, did he divulge the 'Burton snatch' to be the dry, slightly sulphurous aroma of the local beer. Indeed, Burton's water has a higher sulphate content than any other major brewing hub on the planet. Add tip-top amounts of both calcium and magnesium, and low levels of sodium and bicarbonate and the result, having chucked in malted barley, hops, and yeast, is incomparable.

In beer or even boringly unadulterated the water has proved a stimulant to Staffordshire's number two footie team. Burton Albion, 'The Brewers', kicking-off in their yellow and black stripes against Aston Villa in the Championship used to be the stuff of fantasy. Their rise in what I had thought a rugger town has been meteoric. The team only formed in 1950 to hoof about Birmingham & District League. In the trio of Staffordshire clubs they are after Stoke City's shirttails and Port Vale are left playing catch up.

It really is some water!

Long, long ago, when the countryside was split between Anglo-Saxons, Danes and Celts, a wandering Irish nun from Armagh discovered it after an undocumented vision had brought her to a halt. Whatever she believed to have seen happened at Scalpcliffe Hill, these days a nature reserve of ancient woods full of wild garlic, dog's mercury, and scurrying things. Enraptured by the surroundings she dallied for years. Her name was Modwen. Her legacy was four churches, a well, and … something of great significance.

Set in the River Trent at the spot of the 'chariot' bother was 'Andrew's Isle' – the Anglo-Saxons called it 'Andressey', like the iron bridge but spelt with an extra 's'. Anthony finds it rare for Burtoners to make the connection. Anyway, legend has it Modwen cured a dying boy using nowt but prayer and the restorative water drawn from the well sunk at her new home.

The boy, despite never gaining rude health, became King Alfred the Great. Oh, the irony. The Irish had helped create England. To rub it in, Modwen was made a saint. Her soul entering heaven around 900AD her body was eventually buried on 'Andressey'.

A decade or so after the Norman Conquest Alfred's great-great-grandson Wulric Spott founded an abbey in Modwen's honour and named it 'Byrtune'. Modwen was dug up and put inside. Then the monks got brewing and set the precedent.

By 1310, monks, ignoring hangovers, claimed the abbey to be the smallest and poorest Benedictine monastery in the realm. A happy place though, it attracted tradespeople. A tidy bridge was built across the Trent. More folk came. A town blossomed. Byrtune became Burton. And blimey, some bad luck followed.

A fire all but destroyed the town in 1255. Within seventy years Thomas,

Earl of Lancaster burned it again for good measure. A hooligan, he got beheaded. Largely for heckling Edward the Second.

A trio of floods – 1514, 1771 and 1792 – swamped the town to wading point. February 1795 saw Burton entirely drowned following a severe winter:

"On Monday Jan 26th Fahrenheit's Thermometer was at 30 or Freezing Point, others at 23 & some lower. The Rivers Trent and Tame were frozen over, the Corn-Mills unable to Grind, Wheat sold at 9s per strike. A great Flood succeeded upon the Thaw on Tuesday February 10th On which day, great Damage was done by the amazing Quantity of Ice and Waters…"

Staffordshire Record Office.

The floods heralded a hurricane. Then an earthquake is said to have "engaged Dr Darwin's attention". The doctor was Erasmus, Charles Darwin's grandpa. *The Natural History of Staffordshire* records the quake "was felt at Burton, Lichfield, Tutbury, and Repton, in a very sensible manner".

And after further flooding woes, in blew lost zeppelins. Their Great War German bombs not meant for Burton at all blasted one holy mess.

In 1944 an underground munitions store went whoomph. A huge crater resulted, seventy people 'bought it', and the reservoir banks burst causing an outpouring of gloopy sludge.

I suppose everyday dangers of trolley chariots are a minor worry.

Stoicism is a prerequisite.

The Anglo-Saxon Lady Godiva bearing up for example. I'm on about Godiva, wife of Leofric, Earl of Mercia, who rode naked through the streets of Coventry to protest against her hubby's taxes on his tenants. She had good cause for a horse. She actually lived a score and half miles away at a manor in Branston now properly famous for its pickle.

Mrs Graham and her two daughters, Miss Evelyn and Miss Ermentrude, invented the cold platter relish at Branston Lodge in 1922. Chopping small they bunged into pans whatever aged in the larder – swede, carrots, onions, cauliflower, and gherkins were pickled in a simmered sauce of vinegar, tomato, apple dates, agreeably spiced with mustard, coriander, garlic, cinnamon, pepper, cloves, nutmeg, cayenne pepper, and lashings of sugar.

Into mass production it went. The factory, beautifully symmetrical and very classical in style, was intended for machine guns. Crosse & Blackwell, however, pledged to turn it into the largest and best equipped food-preserving plant in the British Empire. 'Bring out the Branston' said the advert. One of the Top 50 UK brands of the twentieth century was the vote. The factory's characteristic brick border wall still dominates much of the Branston Road. While the 'Branston' brand has been sold to the Burntwood-based Japanese food firm Mizkan, for ninety-two and a half million quid.

Getting in a pickle himself, Edward Wightman is a less familiar name. A

Burton textile trader, he believed in soul-sleep, which is to imply our souls either cease to exist or nod off after death rather than being immortal.

Well-respected and a faithful community leader, he was tagged as a Puritan and stubbornly held to principles of expressive freedom. So very Staffie, and in his case most unwise. The religious establishment led by King James the First had their gander up. Edward was the last man to be burned for heresy in Britain.

Tied to the stake in Lichfield market square, fires licking, fair play Edward's courage left him. Hotly crying out to recant he was pulled "well scorched" from the flames. A fortnight later he was brought afresh before the court and was expected to say sorry. Obstinately, he "blasphemed more audaciously than before." The court got stroppy. On 11 April 1612, he was "carried again to the stake where feeling the heat of the fire again would have recanted, but for all his crying the sheriff told him he should cost him no more and commanded faggots to be set to him whence roaring, he was burned to ashes." That was 1612.

More recently, bald and leather-jacketed, and dubbed Faster Pastor by *Bike Magazine*, a former Glasgow shipyard worker can arrange for Hells Angels to be cremated too. In fact he'll deliver them to the curtain with their boots. Patience though is required. Because of preservatives gobbled in modern life, a body burns slower than in Edward's day.

Yet Elim Pentecostal Church was reaching out. A witty poster of theirs in Burton's Moor Street caught Robbie Coltrane's attention when filming his TV series *B-Road Britain*. "Biker Service", it said. "All motorcycle enthusiasts welcome. Your first bike service of the summer free!"

Inside, windowsills were designated helmet parks. Removed pews allowed two rows of twenty-six "gleaming, lovingly polished" motorbikes standing room. Among three score parishioners mingled the 'Coffin Scratchers', a band of hairy, leather-clad bikers. Not a typical congregation.

Stepping down from the pulpit the Reverend Paul Sinclair did more than tend his flock in this life. He has had motorbike sidecars converted to hearses. A Suzuki Hayabusa powered one such. Capable of 247 miles per hour it broke the record for fastest hearse, winning 'Best Modern Hearse' at the 'Hearse of the Year' awards in 2004. Success enough to ponder tandem and hearse for the Lycra-clad cyclist.

Robbie continues to follow the bonnet of his Carmen-red Jag XK150S. Had he done so past the Elim church to as far as the road went he would have arrived at the abbey. Only now it's a swish wine bar whose terrace overlooks Peel's Cut.

Wine? A local fad, surely. Anyway, Burton beer is extra medicinal. Quacks laudably doused 'scorbutic diseases' – those nasty skin and eye complaints – with 'Modwen's Well' water as late as the seventeenth century. Now a brewery uses the water for beer. Those old monks knew a thing or two.

One Burton brewer remains dominant: Molson Coors. The American firm originally came to Burton to take over all of Bass. Oddly, the Belgian brewer Interbrew actually walked off with the 'Bass' name and rights to the world-famous Bass red triangle.

Coors wasted no time obliterating all the triangle's traces. The Bass national brewing museum got renamed as the Coors Visitors Centre. In the stables shire horses Jed and Walter had their dray pimped. The Coors-branding was silliness unto itself. Probably best accept the new tag: The National Brewery Centre.

Noticing beginnings of a slur I thought a ploughman's might soak up the Marston's. Not just with Anthony and Marmy in mind did I order plenty of cheese with the pickle. There was the ancestral heritage to consider.

Anthony then dropped a bombshell. He and Marmy were definitely moving to Repton. Gawd's teeth, that meant ... Derbyshire. I asked if he was suffering from a temperature or mid-life crisis. Neither, he said. Blighty's oldest documented person lived in Repton. Marmy was getting on. Anthony couldn't bear the thought of being parted. The chariot and swan was the last straw. Repton offered sanctuary to "keep her ticking".

What with his decision and my nose dribbling from Marmy's nuzzlings faith in medicinal beer had suddenly gone for a Burton.

Dunstall Hall fading into end titles Romi flipped through TV channels and settled for a programme about big cats. Again interest surged in me until realising I didn't recognise any of the scenery.

LESSON SIXTEEN

Teapot and Radish

*"Come, let us have some tea and continue
to talk about happy things."*
Chaim Potok, American Jewish author.

Fruitlessly, I had wound through the gorgeous Churnet Valley, Staffs 'Little Switzerland'. Hereabouts, one village had entered local folklore in a story about heavy metal. Oakamoor. The name Thomas Bolton will nowadays induce little more than a shrug from Joe Public. In 1858, however, he became an instant legend. Utilising the local resource at his Oakamoor copper works, Thomas manufactured, with considerable help from his workforce, the wire for the first transatlantic telegraph cable. Coil upon coil upon coil. Mindboggling lengths. Good thing Oakamoor boasted the transport convenience of the new-fangled railways. On 16 August, 1858 the first official telegram passed between continents. The ninety-eight words sent by Queen Victoria to President James Buchanan took a mere sixteen hours to send. Terrific stuff. A pity then, that after four years of arduous labour, the cable only lasted three paltry weeks before it frazzled and fried. Excessive voltage the cause in an age of experiment. It was a very expensive telegram. Comprehension requires a degree of mental adjustment.

I though wasn't hunting for copper. I was on the look out for pine martens – rare cat-sized relatives of badger and weasel, chocolate-brown with a creamy-white chest patch. One had found itself photographed in a Consall tree. Another was seen closer to Leek. So I still had hope.

Pulling Milami into a moorlands pot-holed puddle-rut lay-by I buttoned-down the window. Breathing in the fresh air I remembered relationships. Like coarse Carboniferous sandstone to Roaches Grit. Or Wild John and Liz. Faults and fractures to the Goyt Syncline? That I quite forget.

It cannot be helped. Roaches have unappealing connotations. In Australia they are called cockies. I called an evasive one Herbert just so I could tolerate it. In Staffs they hide in fog and mist, their names reminiscent. Garrotting Stone and Hanging Stone, for instance.

I blame the French. They are the ones to call rocks 'roches'. The Gallic spelling for the jutting rocky ridge above Leek was used up until about a century ago. Maps in Keele University's geology department proved it. But why the French? Because it worked with 'Staffordshire terrier'?

1980. Liz quit her monologue about Ezra her maidenhair fern and got involved. We put bounce into every step of 'Brass in Pocket'. Subtle as if she were an on-heat otter, languorously lingering on "I'm special", Liz would have made sassy Chrissie Hynde proud. Wild John beat out the tempo on the back of Liz's seat, an excuse to smell her dark, tousled hair.

Packed in a minibus that jerked and strained along the A53, the wild and unpredictable stretch of peaks and troughs between Leek and Buxton, we spied a pig and a unicorn. And we ten field-tripping students in this land of illusion cheered seeing the 'eye' of the Winking Man wink – the result of a Ramshaw Rocks parallax – a hole that catches and loses the empty sky. Wild John offered a pearl in Liz's ear: "The eye's gleam apparently helps damsels get pregnant." It earned him an "F-off".

Liz should never have encouraged him during the hoot of getting the Devil off our backs. Some of us huddled damp, nursing scuff injuries. The cause? Scrabbling under the Bawdstone – a bloody great boulder balanced on three rocklets lonely on open moor near the steep gritstone cliff of Hen Cloud. Nobly Wild John had flung down his anorak for Liz to crawl upon. That clinched him the coquettish curtsy of hope and brought out his inner chimp.

Once the boulder was whitewashed annually in purification. And as late as the 1940s fit people of Leek joined a procession to pay a visit. I learned, contrary to belief, the stone is not a man-made dolmen, nor does touching it have the healing power to cure a hangover. Local life though needed purpose. Indeed, many a rock is tampered with. One randomly has carved steps to enable a flagpole be put in a hole on the top. Others bear inscriptions. Like those immortalizing the Princess of Teck or Burke, a mutt "faithful as woman braver than man".

Air dank and clouds low, enshrouding, Hen Cloud looked foul. No seeing as far as Cheshire, nor Wales and Snowdon to the west, nor Winter Hill in Lancashire to the north. Not that day. Out of interest, the cliff is responsible for a phenomenon first recorded by Robert Plot, the seventeenth century naturalist: the 'Double Sunset'. Happening on or around the summer solstice it occurs when the sun sets behind Hen Cloud, and soon partially reappears in the hollow of its steep northern side, before setting again. It's all there in Plot's book *The Natural History of Staffordshire*.

The cliff obviously appealed to Brady and Hindley, the Moors Murderers. A dark photo of it was amongst Hindley's clobber after her death.

At our next stop a curlew turned its long down-curved bill away from us, called plaintively, and took wing. Once a common sight across the Staffordshire Moorlands the bird's numbers have declined almost to the wallaby level.

We cast looks around the brackish and supposedly bottomless Black Mere. Natives think of it as the 'Mermaid Pool'. A malicious water nymph lives in it, the gullible say. The story goes a perfectly mortal beauty rebuffed the advances of a local chap. A typical bloke he was unable to accept the rejection and accused his fancy of being a witch. Convinced, a jeering mob drowned her in Black Mere. There were repercussions. You just need to read the inscribed rhyme in the nearby 'Mermaid' pub to learn the outcome.

> "She calls on you to greet her
> Combing her dripping crown,
> And if you go to greet her,
> She ups and drags you down..."

Livestock refuse to drink Black Mere's water and birds seem never to fly across it. Blooming heck, I can to attest to a black-eyed crow making a detour. Or was a strong wind gust?

And the pool bottomless? My arse! At its deepest point the water is no more than 6-foot. And it has a muddy floor. In wet suit and flippers, plus aqualung, Philip Davis of Stoke-on-Trent, a committee member of the British Sub-Aqua Club, North Staffordshire branch, discovered that much.

Yet the pool level has its mystery, particularly in a hot summer. During a grass blaze the Fire Brigade pumped out ninety thousand gallons. The Fire Chief was adamant the level hardly varied. Mercifully no thingamabob appeared threatening to flood Leek and Leekfrith as it apparently did in the mid nineteenth century. Those who 'witnessed' that event repaired to the Mermaid's bar, a leisurely ten-minute stroll away with their story.

A secret water source does likely exist connecting Black Mere and nearby 'Doxey Pool'. The second-mentioned is worthy of remark. It ripples cold and brooding high atop a Roaches craggy outcrop where fluff-top cotton grass, spongy moss, and spiky reeds grow. The name Doxey is not reference, as some think to a prostitute, but to a common mediaeval predator: the itinerant bag lady – fortune-teller, quack, and, aptly in light of Hen Cloud, chicken stealer, all rolled into one.

Doxey's, too, has its balderdash. Cogitating along lines of the Lorelei, folk like to believe the pool's haunted by the granddaughter of cavern-dwelling highwayman 'Bower of the Rocks'. His cavern, very near Doxey Pool, was called Rock Hall. Rock falls created the roof, sides and entrance. Bower sheltered smugglers and deserters.

The granddaughter vanished without trace and was much missed. By all accounts she had a gorgeous voice and sang "sadly to herself songs that sounded foreign to English ears". A lass with a talent other than highway robbery and surrounded by desperate men would probably have sought a civilised stage without wood-spoked wheels and horses.

The legend amongst us students was Andy. He waggled two fingers above his head and then made hopping motions. His wasn't a bad impression. We all laughed. Liz's laugh was loudest. But we wanted to see a real wallaby. Eventually, years later, I did. It bounced across the narrow and bumpy-surfaced Acheron highway into the tree ferns of Australia's State of Victoria, naturally as far removed from Staffordshire's high pools and heather as I could envisage.

Taking in the view across open moor and into the wooded valleys below it was hard to believe the Potteries were so close. Ten minutes and you are out of them. 'Hod', Burslem born Bernard Hollowood, knew the benefits. Being "deep in the moorlands" nourished him.

Here was a man who played cricket for Staffordshire in the '30s and '40s. He had Sydney Barnes as a teammate and frivolously scripted an article titled 'Sawdust'. According to his autobiography, Hod "allowed (my) pen to consider in mock-serious language the advantages and disadvantages of various timbers as sources of material."

This 'scholarly discourse' on the subtleties of wicket preparation was promptly dispatched to Sir Pelham Warner, the editor of *Cricketer* who published it.

Hod writes: "To this day I believe that he (Warner) accepted it as a genuine and constructive examination of a hitherto neglected item in the paraphernalia of the game. There may in fact be groundsmen operating today with my article as their Bible, groundsmen who talk seriously to their saw-mill suppliers of the virtues of elm sawdust, the reliability of ash and the absorbing quality of sycamore."

Cricket aside, Hod lectured in economics at the Stoke-on-Trent's School of Commerce, and became the ninth editor of *Punch* magazine in the '60s. He brought his acerbic wit to bear on the British character:

"We are an odd lot, a people cradled in the past to such an extent that we enjoy the mystical titular rule of the monarchy, and all the ceremony and trappings that go with it, and still look with awe upon the faces of nitwits labelled with cherished surnames and titles – and at the same time we are a people who subscribe passionately to the tenets of democracy."

One of those 'nitwits', his family's money made in the Macclesfield silk factories, was Lieutenant Colonel Henry Courtney Brocklehurst, 10th Royal Hussars and Royal Flying Corps pilot. He liked to be called Courtney and got appointed Game Warden of the Sudan. Well, he kind of had the CV. If that had an omission like as not no one dobbed.

His brother Sir Philip of Swythamley Hall owned the Roaches and the surrounding land. In the 1930s London Zoo feared an outbreak of lurgy.

Courtney being a member of the Zoological Society had jolly good wheeze: build a small reserve at Roches Hall at Upper Hulme. That way, the lucky would survive. Invites were dispatched. Three yaks, one Nilgai antelope, and some wallabies turned up, of which five promptly escaped – enough for a breeding population.

Wallabies are elusive. And over the years there have been many 'sightings'. Hares must accept their share of responsibility. However, unable to bounce or hide, paw cut on a broken bottle, a wallaby was actually found during the 1980s. A man of character stumbled on it. Black eye patch, ratty bearded, and rough clothed, Doug Moller was known as 'Lord of the Roaches'. The animal died from septicaemia in his arms.

The loss, a massive blow to the wallaby population, was also a blow to Doug. He cherished nature. Choosing to escape run-a-long-a-ding-ding modern life he had bought revamped but dilapidated Rock Hall for a snip.

Made a gamekeeper's cottage with arched lattice-frame windows by Sir Philip, the highwayman's cave was incorporated into the kitchen. Stationed to catch poachers the last abiding gamekeeper reputedly raised twelve nippers. Perhaps this was Doug's inspiration for potential.

Doug had much to cope with. His number one role was as loving carer to his invalid wife Annie. And somehow he managed. No plumbing existed, let alone sanitation. No electricity. No gas. The 'front door' was only a gaping hole. Climbers peeing in his water supply and loosing rocks to crack the roof slates were his bugbear. As, too, were vandals. They did for his generator. A health inspector from Staffordshire Moorlands district council declared Rock Hall: "unfit for human habitation".

A log fire giving warmth and light, Doug and Annie remained resilient. Twenty-seven quid a week social security only covered so much. Awaking once to six inches of snow on their bed wasn't a surprise. They survived for years in this fashion before finally selling up in 1990. But not before *National Geographic* immortalised Doug silhouetted in the night blue light of a snow-silent skeletal wood. A penny though for his thoughts, Rock Hall has since been renamed 'Don Whillans Hut', a bivouac for climbers named in memory of a notable mountaineer. Hopefully one well mannered.

Wallabies irrefutably seeming non-existent, democratically, in a nod to Hod, we students unanimously voted for second best: a pub.

We got overruled. "Next Three Shire Heads," Bill our totalitarian tutor said. "To Flash," he added.

Getting arrested wasn't Bill's intention. To park the minibus in the highest inhabited village in England was. A circling buzzard mewed us greeting.

In Staffordshire's attic, 1514 feet above sea level, hillside-hugging Flash is remote. Though the area had a large number of coal pits dating back to 1401

and today sustains the country's highest shop – Flash Bar Stores – the village is really just about black-faced, wool-scraggy Swaledale sheep and farmers, and … the Teapot Club. Hard to believe such a little set was touched by the monstrous ego that was Robert Maxwell, the pension plunderer. He, the publisher of the *Daily Mirror*, *Sunday Mirror*, the *People*, *Daily Record*, *New York Daily News* and a raft of titles elsewhere across the world plus several book publishers, including Macmillan.

How come? Well, the Teapot Club has its roots in money saving. People would put aside their spare coppers. An elected committee made regular collections and all proceeds were kept in a large teapot to be divvied out to villagers in times of unemployment, sickness or bereavement. And like a Friendly Society, each year they would have a church service and then a banner led parade. The Flash Rose Queen would smile and wave and the local brass band played its heart out. In the mid 1990s all this had to stop.

Maxwell committing a massive fraud by plundering his employees' pension funds in order to shore up his companies resulted in new laws on savings organisations. Even the small amounts rattled by the Teapot Club couldn't legally be collected. 1995 saw the last pukka Flash Teapot Service and parade.

Villagers determined revival. Quickly the service and parade became custom with an added extra, a well dressing – the floral decoration of a well originally linked with the belief in water deities. Well dressings are big in these parts. More than six thousand visitors attend at Endon. Designs created from flower petals usually follow a theme. In 2015 it was the eight hundredth anniversary of Magna Carta.

The Flash teapot that goes walkabout borne on a rudimentary litter is now a hugely symbolic papier mâché affair of blue painted hoops and tall as a man. An accordion and fiddle do the work of the band. The Rose Queen has kept her retinue and the homemade banners are ever colourful. With the rag-tag procession's goal being the Traveller's Rest pub at Flash Bar a mile away, the danger of bemusing drivers on the A53 is allayed by officialdom closing the road.

Flash in the past was off-limits for wholly different reasons. It had a … reputation. For funny money. Hell, counterfeiting was rife. The village's very name associates itself with anything that is dishonest or non genuine.

And here, on the exposed spaces, 'badgers' squatted. Not the aforementioned pine marten relative that's worm eating and whose hair's made into shaving brushes. No, no. To be a badger hereabouts was to be a peddler, and as rough as the landscape. Nobody batted an eyelid at the prize fighting and cock fighting. The attracted unsavoury crowds offered the badgers opportunity.

Reputedly a court was held on this spot in the fourteenth century by order of the Black Prince but it proved pointless. And the law continued to be frustrated. Police, only allowed to act within their own county limits, could not follow lawbreakers or coiners once they had covered the rugged mile to Three Shire Heads, crossed the stone-arched packhorse bridge, and chosen between Cheshire and Derbyshire.

Over stile after stile we went. Across boggy ground through reed grass and steadily down into the Dane Valley. Rabbits, rabbits. Then a footbridge and stream-dipping wagtails. Passed a farm and a boulder littered slope. Another farm. At last a signpost. A squidgy path between bracken and gorse. Passed yellow suns of coltsfoot. Right first fork, left at the second, and onwards until the sound of burble and bubble and waterfall tumble: the River Dane. The river's name is from the Old Welsh *dafn*, meaning ' tickle'. Ah, very sweet. And a useless piece of gen Wild John was aware of. Liz coped being a water-splashed giggle-bundle decently enough.

Hurrah, though, we had arrived at Staffordshire's most northern point. Fed by a streamlet rippled the Panniers Pool. Here slung with baskets and saddlebags ponies in days of yore quenched their thirst and hardy mortals swam.

Knackered, I collapsed on a huge rock slab of millstone grit – "a hard sofa" Andy called it. We shook heads at Wild John and Liz pratting about on the packhorse bridge, him now goading her with an alderfly. The entertainment was short lived. An ominous chrisom of mist descending the beeches and pines above soon had us all moving again.

Anyway, tutor Bill's despotic whip cracked. The Black Forest awaited us. We still had to note Lud's Church, the 'Green Chapel' of Arthurian legend where the Green Knight lost his head to Sir Gawain in a yearly ritual. Once back in the minibus it was a short spin to the car park beside the youth hostel, an ex-silk mill, at Gradbach.

I have to say it, this tiny hamlet was a hotbed of disrepute just as bad if not worse than Flash. At first glance Gradbach would have appeared respectable. Silk weaving and button making were its cottage industries from 1640 for two hundred years. The button presses though had a dual purpose – popping out fake coins. The work of a single gang, hanging of a few of their number at Chester proved dissuasive. However, in all likelihood the Flash counter-feiters stock was based on them making hay copying the button press prac-tice.

Gradbach though won on the ghoulishness stakes. Overgrown founda-tions are what remain of a demolished cottage, once home to a family of stomach-churning villainy. Thanks to a Flash badger's tip-off they were arrested. The charges? Several counts of murder and cannibalism. Wow.

From the minibus our aching legs hadn't far to traipse.

Lud's Church entrance is modest. A bit of a squeeze, in fact. Neither does the first chamber impress. But down some poignantly worn steps and blimey, there was room for several hundred souls, or should I say heretics.

In truth the 'Chapel', over a hundred yards long, is a naturally deep doglegged cleft in the rock. Slippage of a large mass of Roaches Grit slightly downhill into the Dane Valley is the cause. Apart from the lumpy leaf-mould carpet assuredly it's very green. The 50-foot scarped sides are mossy and profusely lichened. Grasses drip. Ferns cling. And Liz suggested it the perfect place her Ezra might like a holiday.

That was until she heard of Trafford's Leap. For sure locals once knew the cleft by the name, such was the cautionary tale of Sir Trafford, a former Squire of Swythamley. Out on horseback hunting with his hound pack he strayed at a jolly old canter much too close to the herbage-hidden edge of Lud's Church. Sir Trafford got lucky. His nag chanced on a jumpable gap. The running hounds though hadn't the reach and plunged to their tangled end.

Andy's exaggerated howling noises got ignored. To regain our attention he put his hands together in prayer and began muttering gibberish – a presumptuous attempt at being a Lollard. It seems Lud's Chapel takes its name from a Lollard preacher. Walter de Lud-Auk, a fourteenth century follower of John Wycliffe, to be exact. Lollard belief that the Bible should be available in the language of the common people threatened the State's existence. And demanding the Church set the example to folk to live a life of scriptural poverty didn't improve matters.

Thus Walter used the ravine as a religious but secret gathering place. John of Gaunt had sheltered Wycliffe and the Lollards before he went chasing the Crown of Castille. After he left it became open season. The Lollards were quickly damned as heretics.

As the chasm was on his land Sir Philip Brocklehurst, blessed with imagination and astutely business-like, had an asset to exploit. A popular Victorian tourist attraction emerged with a halfpenny entrance fee. Farmers got in on the act. Their horse-drawn cart decked out in best linen collected the grockles from Leek railway station. It was tangible community spirit.

Placing the figurehead of the sail ship 'Swythamley' in a high Lud's Church niche was a nice touch. What grockles saw was a rum statue. Spooky even. Named 'Lady Lud', it commemorated the death of Walter's daughter, Alice. Or so Sir Philip had folk believe. His story of Walter being captured at a meeting had further embellishment. Alice, mistakenly shot in the raid, now haunted the place.

Not that any of us gave a fiddler's fart.

The atmosphere of Traveller's Rest pub was in stark contrast to the wet coolness of Lud's Church. Peat fires smouldered and the most 'draft' beers anywhere in Blighty awaited our selections, though teapot paraders were absent as wallabies.

Tutor Bill hummed Blue Oyster Cult's 'Don't Fear the Reaper'.

❖ ❖ ❖

The score in my Moleskine read: Pine Martens nil. Wallabies nil. And Leek, 'Queen of the Moorlands', offered nil McDonalds, which was largely Liz's reason for choosing to live in a town awaiting the arrival of steam trains. The Churnet Valley Railway really was hoping to push the extra mile from Leek-brook.

I had half an hour to kill before meeting up with her and sampling her recommendation: pistachio and rosebud cake. I somehow needed to broach the delicate subject of now not so Wild John and put the world to rights.

Behind a veggie laden trestle table the loud blokish voice at Leek's open-air market was 'sarf-east', likely London. "Spuds pound a bag! C'mon ladies and gents. Oranges pound a bag! Lovely oranges! I'm giving them away!" A white van had its doors wide open. Inside were boxes on boxes.

Some contained bunched leaf-limp radishes rubber-banded together. I scrutinised them. None appeared haunted. But you can never be too careful in Leekbrook. Not since the story of the radish that talked, the fault of hen-pecked Robert Emerson. Early in the nineteenth century he was the church-warden at St. Edwards, the sizable mediaeval edifice in Church Street. His difficult wife Ann whimsically demanded he grew her some radishes out of season. Such a chore needed the very best compost. But where should he find it? Ah, thought Robert, a grave. Ann got her radishes.

Of these she chose the plumpest. Just before having its bottom nibbled the radish screamed:

"Please don't bite off my tail.
The top of my legs, and arms I bewail,
But Please Madame Ann, don't dare bite off my tail!"

Oh my word, the soul of the deceased had become veg and pleaded to be reburied where dug. It's said, Ann never ate radish again. I suspect Robert a rather sly ventriloquist. But that's just me. His gravestone without sign of vegetables around is findable in St Edward's churchyard.

"Caulis a pound each!" The greengrocer glanced at his watch…. "Caulis fifty pence!"

There was a canny digging in Staffie purses and pockets. Folk raised their bums off bright-coloured benches. Okay, their iron red-combed, black fowl armrests are very nice. The council, however, had ordered moorhens. Also black, these sport a red facial shield. The cock-up over a crackly telephone in 1956 is simple to understand. "More hens?" … "Absolutely!"

A bearded, florid-cheeked chap in wide-brimmed hat launched into a rant. "You're all locusts. Locusts! In the Lord's name repent!" For good measure cardboard string-tied to his rattletrap bicycle quoted biblically: "The locusts have no king, yet all of them march in rank. Proverbs 30:27."

I scooted past and got lucky in the indoor market. Not all had yet tramped off with the oatcakes from the waxen old codger selling them in polythene bags from under a cheese counter. Always selling out "eventually", he had no need to lower his prices.

I found Liz fending off the wagging club-clipped tail of an unknown large poodle. The Sprout Café is an arty place. Perhaps a tad too bohemian. The loo has a glass door. The tables are shabby chic and Earl Grey, or any tea for that matter, is served in mismatching china. Liz said this was trendy. Avant-garde was the latest fad in café culture. Blimey, Leek. Only a short while before-hand the ambition of a fifteen-year-old mum of maybe one day working on the Morrisons deli counter hit the front page of the *Leek Post and Times*.

Doing best to ignore what had turned into a wrestling match between poodle and a lady in ethnic bandana, Liz sighed. "Having the P and R cake? Think I'll have the carrot muffin."

"Make that two," I said. "The thunder cloud you're under could turn Leek dark."

Liz almost snarled. "The District Council is needing garlic and wolfsbane to ward off McDonalds who are worse than that dog with the bloody bacon. They've bunged in yet another new planning application. What'll come first, Staffs suffering HS2 or Leek having a Maccy D 'drive-thru'?"

"Nip and tuck," I said, unhelpfully; keeping thoughts to myself of the effect thousands of persuasive tourists chuffing into town by the carriage-load might have.

"If Maccy D's win I'm moving to Eccleshall and I'll get a licence to crenel-late myself like its castle did."

"You'd better tell John. He's still calling you Teapot Liz. It's weird every-body seems on the brink of upping sticks. Anthony's already left the county. Anna's finally accepted Stewy's bog snorkelling fetish and toot sweet they are both off across Offa's Dyke. Mark's set on civilising Greenwich. Ejaz has flabbergasted himself and got a job in New Zealand where they still accept you even in mid-life, whereas Australia's little better than a problematic *Logan's Run*. Big news is Rodge is deserting Bentilee. He and Dyta are an item and Coventry bound. They're a perfect match, mind. She eats his borsch and she's fattening him up on pierogi."

"Sometimes Wild John makes me feel fettered as the chained oak." Liz bemoaned, alluding to the fabled tree that triggered the Alton Towers dark ride 'Hex'. Should ever I think of it, a fubsy braless young miss with a ginger scrape-back and hooped earrings hippo-ing aboard comes to mind. On the butt of her straining jeans 'Kiss Me' was in spangles. I had spun on my heels traumatised and never returned.

Up a set of steps, the oak, its exposed roots mossy, is brittle and splintered nowadays. Chains dangle. It's 400 yards down a woodland footpath known as the Barbary Gutter, which runs from opposite the 'Chained Oak' B&B, converted stables close to Alton Towers main entrance.

The Earl of Shrewsbury was returning home to a very different Alton Towers on an autumn night in 1821. On the road in front of the already venerable tree was an old beggar, either man or woman depending on the story's version.

Halting the Earl the beggar scrounged for a coin. Brutishly dismissed the beggar spat a curse: For every falling branch a member of the Earl's family would die. That same night a storm blew, a limb fell, and a family member of the Earl's snuffed it. Next morning he ordered his servants to iron chain every bough, making them fall proof. However, spring 2007 had a branch tumble. An iron link had rusted through. The family did a head count. No one had croaked. The old tree stays unmoved, a true Staffs survivor.

I knew the same of Liz.

"Chained Oak?" I said, "Yeah, yeah, as if. Honestly Liz, you're free as a starling. John's like putty in your wings and he's pining in Stafford. Please, ignore its Maccy Ds and sort things out the two of you." A flowery china teapot of Darjeeling arrived. Now, where were those muffins?

The poodle decided to lovingly bonk my leg.

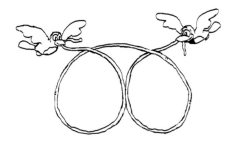

Postscript

"The secret to creativity is knowing how to hide your sources."
Albert Einstein, physicist.

1 May 2016. The first Staffordshire Day. A celebration of "everything that's great about our county," the county's official Tourist Board posted on the Web.

Judging by the kerfuffle in a Banksia shrub pairs of sparrows tied the knot. Waiting to cross the six-lane highway that cuts between Ali's and my Melbourne flat and the Moorabbin second-hand bookshop I had time to reflect. The thrum of traffic, the wind in the eucalypts, and a green and crimson squadron of screaming lorikeets didn't overly distract me pondering what makes Staffordshire special.

Kind hearts and spirits? Crikey, yes. Burntwood's Malarkeys? Too right. Burslem's sadly departed Lemmy of Motorhead? Quite possibly. Pedigree ale? Without a doubt. A Wedgwood Portland Vase sitting in a National Gallery of Victoria glass display cabinet? Absolutely.

I also thought of contemporary creative minds – the ones of ordinary bods undeterred by difficulty. The Stoke City flag floating in space, and white, life-saving bags on Cannock Chase wooden posts didn't just happen by themselves.

The floaty flag was a Christmas treat for Potters' fans dreamt up after a few beers. Backslaps have been earned by Andy Rushton, a bloke coping with multiple sclerosis. His wacky 'Let's Get Stoke in Space' campaign cajoled Brit astronaut Tim Peake to do the necessary with the club's colours in the International Space Station. Bringing flag and spaceman together was elaborate. The former launched from the United States folded away amongst seven thousand three hundred pounds of cargo. Tim blasted off from Kazakhstan and needed to rummage before writing on Twitter: "Happy Christmas @jolly-happybore (Rushton) – you did it!!" Loud cheers were heard in amongst Melbourne's Stoke City supporters branch. What they think of the Britannia Stadium being renamed the bet365 Stadium is another matter, altogether. Some think it's a gamble.

Of course the flag was not the first Staffie object in space. A piece of rock from Darwin's Dyke travelled on the MIR space station from February 1998 to February 1999. The rock's donator, Staffordshire astronomer Phil Parker, wrote explanatory words for its plaque:

"This piece of Dolerite rock is from the Butterton igneous dyke near Newcastle-under-Lyme, UK. This dyke was discovered in c. 1842 by Charles Darwin, famous scientist and author of *On The Origin Of Species* ... It is hoped that this token of our millennium will act as a focus for inspiration to descendants of our generation and species to continue the exploration of space with possibility of meeting extra terrestrial species and discovering their origins."

I just wonder if any alien will understand "wy shall bey stuck 'ere aw dee" or "thee knowst wot ar meyn, dustna?" But, how could I forget. ETs had been through all that in Stafford.

The white bags? Well okay, the initial idea is Yank, but for once nothing to do with social media, fried chicken, or duck-billed caps. It's the application that's important.

During 2015 a hundred and sixty-three Cannock Chase deer got car-clobbered. The solution was creative, pure and simple. At intervals along a pretty and busy stretch of road large white canvas bags were popped over wooden post tops. Cheap and effective. So very Staffordshire. Bag and post deter deer herds from the hard track and keeps them in the woods. Nobody quite knows why it works. But it does. Don't knock it. Bigfoot's not been seen lately either.

In Stafford at present Liz's Brown Betty teapot is cobweb free and she has gone onto iTunes and downloaded 'Wuthering Heights'. She listens to it occasionally watching the cat paw salmon sachet content into the vinyl version's grooves. Wild John slurps tea blissfully from his "Cost kick a bo agen a wo an yed it till it bosts" mug. As far I was aware their Facebook status is stable.

The highway finally crossed, a bookshelf browse among the webs of potentially dangerous spiders had an outcome that was four dollars and immaculate – former Keelite Marina Lewycka's third novel *We Are All Made of Glue*. Apt in light of my ruddy Staffordshire attachment.

When all is said and done the Original Mirrors' 'Reflections' is a tune, I guess, only I, and a few, still hum. Strawberry yogurt chicken, meanwhile, has become bewilderingly popular. Ejaz calls it 'Mum's korma'.

Dialect

ar'll come an' sey yer aggen – I'll come and see you again

arm – I'm

Bay Chum Spiders – Beecham's Powders

be aw accynts – by all accounts

bosted clock – miserable face

breakstuff – breakfast

bresses – breasts

brid – bird

bun – constipated

buzzed – late for work

cheer – chair

chimdy – chimney

chonnock – turnip

chopsing – chattering

chunterrin – having a moan

cleowse – close

cod-placer – Experienced foreman who knew how and where the ware should be placed in the bottle oven to get the best fire.

Cost kick a bo against a wo an' then 'it it wi' thi yed till it bosses? – Can you kick a ball against a wall and then hit it with your head until it bursts?

croodle – huddle together

crowline – a straight line (mixture of as the crow flies & bee-line)

cunny-fogle – cunning deceit

dee – day

dine – down

doh-er – door

drumble – hole

'edge-bonk – hedge-bank

fardle – waste time

feasen – hurry

fiddle faddle – trifles

fow staith – false teeth

fried frogs – friend sliced potatoes
gansey – cardigan

goose low – go slow

grey nice – greenhouse

hasky – very dry weather

ice – house

jally-wow – witch

jollyer – the chap putting clay into a revolving plaster mould using a profile tool to shape it.

jiggered – exhausted

kecks – trousers

ki – cow (plural: kine)

kim-wam – to gossip

kine slice – council house

knivy – miserly

ligger – liar

lobby – type of stew

lumpy-tums – porridge

males – meals

messin' abite in weyter – messing about in water

monstink – snob

moudiwarp – mole

mullygrub – to hit

moppet – moth/dark

nar an' aggen – now and again

nazzy – ill-tempered

nesh – cold

nogger – football game

one-legged dancer – the girl working the large wheel that kept the potter's wheel turning had to stand tip-toe high on one leg to reach the top.

orts – food leftovers

owd mon – husband or dad.

pather – pad about like a dog

peffled – speckled

puddled – stupid

pugman – tossed leaves of clay onto the throw

pobs – bread or toast in warm milk or tea

poo – pool

queedle – seesaw

rind abite – roundabout

salary – celery

shardruck – a rubbish tip for broken pottery

slay – sleep

swaller – swallow (bird)

swobsy – fat

They akses t'many questions – you ask too many questions

Thee knowst wot ar meyn, dustna? – You know what I mean, don't you?

th'seyson o' peyce an' goodwill – the season of peace and goodwill.

uptychuck – to bowl a cricket ball using an elevated trajectory

werkin – working

werritin – worrying

wik – week

woke – walk

woots – oats

Wy shall bey stuck 'ere aw dee – We shall be stuck here all day.

yarbs – herbs

yarn – heron

Yone get blowed awee – You'll get blown away

APPENDIX TWO

Extracts from the Stafford Assizes of people from the Stoke-on-Trent area sentenced to 'Transportation to Australia'.

The youngest transported was a ten-year old. The oldest, sixty.

(w = writes, r = reads)

Vernon ABBOTTS, 18 [b. c1804], Trial Place Stafford, 1822.1 Assize. Offence: at Stoke-on-Trent; Theft, quantity of brass metal 'from an engine'. Victim: Marquis of Stafford; Sentence: Transportation, 7 years.

William ASTBURY, 35 [b. c1787], Tr.p. Stafford, 1822.1 Assize. Offence, at Lane End: theft of wearing apparel and shoes from Myatt & Co; Sentence: transportation, 7 years.

William BAGNALL, 27 [b. c1808], Tr.p. Stafford, 1831.1 Assize. Offence, at Stoke-upon-Trent: theft – 1 cotton handkerchief and 10 shillings in copper coin, from John Salt. Sentence: transportation, 7 years. Having been previously convicted of felony. [w; r]

Albert(?) BAILEY, 24 [b. c1811], Tr.p. Stafford, 1835.2 Assize. Offence, at Stoke-upon-Trent: theft – 150 pieces of china, from Thomas Gerrard and others. Sentence: transportation, 7 years. On trial for 2 offences. [w; r]

Arthur BALL, 27 [b. c1793], Tr.p. Stafford, 1820.3 Assize. Offence, at Lane End: theft – cloth or clothing, from William Allen. Sentence: transportation, 7 years.

William BANNISTER, 27 [b. c1812], Tr.p. Stafford, 1839.2 Assize. Offence, at Stoke-upon-Trent: theft – 2 quarts of whiskey, 12 lbs of tea, and other articles, from Thomas Pickford, and another. Sentence: transportation, 10 years. [w; r]

Jeremiah BAYLEY, 21 [b. c1801], Tr.p. Stafford, 1822.1 Assize. Offence, at Burslem: theft – 1 pair of shoes, from Ephraim Meyer. Sentence: T, 7 yrs.

Samuel BAYLEY, 22 [b. c1806], Tr.p. Stafford, 1828.4 Assize. Offence, at Stoke-upon-Trent: theft – chest of tea, from William Wayte. Sentence: T, 7 yrs.

John BENTLEY, 14 [b. c1814], Tr.p. Stafford, 1828.1 Assize. Offence, at Lane End: theft – book, from Charles Watts (shopkeeper); Sentence: T, 7 yrs.

Nathan BENTON, 10 [b. c1819], Tr.p. Stafford, 1829.1 Assize. Offence, at Burslem: theft – watch, from John Lockett. Sentence: T, 7 yrs.

Thomas BETSON, 33 [b. c1799], Tr.p. Stafford, 1832.4 Assize. Offence, at Hanley: theft – 2 frocks, from Isaac Sherwin. Sentence: T, 7 yrs.

John BIRCH, 21 [b. c1799], Tr.p. Stafford, 1820.3 Assize. Offence, at Lane End: theft – 1 pr. breeches, 1 waistcoat, 1 shirt; from William Jervis. Sentence: T, 7 yrs.

William BIRCH, 19 [b. c1800], Tr.p. Stafford, 1819.2 Assize. Offence, at Lane End: theft – tobacco and soap, from Joseph Done; Sentence: T, 7 yrs.

Job CHATTERLEY, 24 [b. c1809], Tr.p. Stafford, 1833.4 assizes; Offence, at Stoke-upon-Trent: theft – 1 basket knife, 2 earthen salt cellars, 24 dozen plates, 30 dishes, and a quantity of other articles, from William Ridgway; Sentence: T, 7 yrs.

Thomas DAVIS, 18 [b. c1813], Tr.p. Stafford, 1831.4 assizes; Offence, at Lane End: theft of a quantity of chinaware, from William Hilditch & Co; Sentence: T, 7 yrs.

Sarah EMERY, 13 [b. c1818], Tr.p. Stafford, 1831.1 assizes; offence, at Lane End: robbery – theft of 2 cheeses, from William Plant; Sentence: T, 7 yrs.

John FALLOWS, 60 [b. c1779], Tr.p. Stafford, 1839.4 assizes; offence, at Lane End: theft of a quantity of iron, from William Hanbury Sparrow; Sentence: T, 7 yrs. [r]. After a previous conviction for felony.

Christopher GIANERA, 36 [b. c1784], Tr.p. Stafford, 1820.4 assizes; offence, at Etruria: theft of brass furniture, other articles, from Josiah Wedgwood; Sentence: T, 7 yrs.

Hannah HAMBLETON, 10 [b.1818], Tr.p. Stafford, 1828.4 assizes; offence, at Hanley: theft of 1 handkerchief, ribbon, and a net collar, from Edith Stevenson; Sentence: T, 7 yrs.

Henry HEATH, 26 [b.1812], Tr.p. Stafford, 1838.3 assizes; offence, at Bucknall: theft of malt, and other articles, from Jeremiah Beardmore; Sentence: T, 7 yrs.

John KENT, 19 [b. c1812], Tr.p. Stafford, 1831.4 assizes; offence, at Lane End: theft – quantity of chinaware, from William Hilditch & Co; Sentence: T, 7 yrs.

John KNIGHT, 18 [b. c1809], Tr.p. Stafford, 1827.1 assizes; offence, at Burslem: theft – hat, from John Tilston (market stallholder); Sentence: T, 7 yrs.

James LITTLEWOOD, 19, [b. c1806], Tr.p. Stafford, 1825.1 assizes; offence, at Burslem: theft – 5 silk handkerchiefs, from Samuel Tunnicliffe; Sentence: T, 7 yrs.

George LOWE, 29 [b. c1810], Tr. p. Stafford, 1839.4 assizes; offence, at Lane End: theft – 1 basket, 1 bag, 91lbs of flour, from John Britton; Sentence: T, 14 yrs. [r].

William MARTIN, 18 [b. c1801], Tr.p. Stafford, 1819.2 assizes; offence, at Lane End: theft – tobacco and soap, from Joseph Done; Sentence: T, 7 yrs;

James NIND, 28 [b. c1802], Tr.p. Stafford, 1830.3 assizes; offence, at Stoke-upon-Trent: theft – 19 hen fowls & 1 cock fowl, from John Smith; Sentence: T, 7 yrs.

John PRITCHARD, 14 [b. c1812], Tr.p. Stafford, 1826.4 assizes; offence, at Hanley: theft – money (5/-), from Jabez Wilson (shopkeeper); Sentence: T, 7 yrs.

John ROBERTS, 22 [b. c1808], Tr.p. Stafford, 1830.2 assizes; offence, at Burslem: theft – 300lbs of lead, fixed to a slip house, from John Riley Marsh and others; Sentence: T, 14 yrs.

John ROBINSON, 19 [b. c1800], Tr.p. Stafford, 1819.3 assizes; offence, at Newcastle: theft – 1 piece of printed cotton, from George Barnes; Sentence: T, 7 yrs.

Joseph SALT, 17 [b. c1816], Tr.p. Stafford, 1833.4 assizes; offence, at Stoke-upon-Trent: theft – 1 silk pocket handkerchief, from James Lindop; Sentence: T, 7 yrs.

Henry SAVERY, 29 [b. c1808], Tr.p. Stafford, 1837.3 assizes; offence, at Stoke-upon-Trent: theft – quantity of iron, from William Hanbury Sparrow; Sentence: T, 7 yrs. [ww; rw].

Alfred SHENTON, 18 [b. c1813], Tr.p. Stafford, 1831.4 assizes; offence, at Lane End: theft – quantity of chinaware, from William Hilditch & Co; Sentence: T, 7 yrs.

James SMITH, 14 [b. c1819], Tr.p. Stafford, 1833.1 assizes; offence, at Stoke-upon-Trent: theft – piece of leather, from John Tabbiner (master); Sentence: T, 7 yrs.

Felix STOKES, 19 [b. c1810], Tr.p. Stafford, 1829.4 assizes; offence, at Stoke-upon-Trent: theft – 12 china teacups, 12 china saucers, 2 china tea pots, and 16 china plates, from Thomas Drewry; Sentence: T, 7 yrs.

John TUNNICLIFFE, 20 [b. c1812], Tr.p. Stafford; 1832.1 assizes; offence, at Burslem: theft- 2 fowls, from George Frederick Bowers; Sentence: T, 7 yrs.

George TWIGG, 23 [b. c1808], Tr.p. Stafford, 1831.1. assizes; offence, at Stoke-upon-Trent: theft – 10 china tea cups, 10 china tea saucers, 1 china tea pot, 1 china sugar bowl, 2 china plates; from Richard Hicks & Partners; Sentence: T, 7 yrs.

John WALTON, 23 [b. c1804], Tr.p. Stafford, 1827.1 assizes; offence, at Hanley: theft of a coat, from John Hancock; Sentence: T, 7 yrs.

Richard WHITEHURST, 21 [b. c1814], Tr.p. Stafford, 1835.1 assizes; offence, at Stoke-upon-Trent: theft of 1 jug, 1lb and a half of treacle, half a pound of soap, 1lb of sugar, 1 basket, and other articles, from Richard Bloor; Sentence: T, 7 yrs. [w; r]. Having been previously convicted of felony.

James WOLFE, 20 [b. c1812], Tr.p. Stafford, 1832.4 assizes; offence, at Lane End: theft – a piece of cheese, from Ralph Baker; Sentence: T, 7 yrs.

Samuel YOXALL, 18 [b. c1810], Tr.p. Stafford, 1828.4 assizes; offence, at Wolstanton: theft – 1 bridle bit and other articles, from Charles Davenport; Sentence: T, 7 yrs.

Omelette Arnold Bennett Recipe

To serve two stout Staffordshire folk, or three not so stout.

The Basics:

For the fish, simmer 200g of smoked haddock in 250ml of milk, drain it and break it into large, juicy flakes.

Use the milk left behind after cooking the haddock to make a white sauce with 40g of butter and three 15ml spoons of flour.

Fold in the flaked haddock and 3 tbsps of finely chopped curly parsley.

Put 30g of butter into an omelette pan. Warm it gently. Then add 6 lightly beaten eggs.

When the omelette is ready, add the sauce, scatter over a small handful of grated Parmesan and grill until bubbling.

Makes one very large, deep omelette, 30cm in diameter, or two smaller ones.

The Trick:

Don't overcook the haddock. In less than ten minutes it's wonderful. Make the haddock sauce before starting the omelette, so it remains nice and fluffy.